I0479471

The Joy Of Coloring

This Book

Belongs To

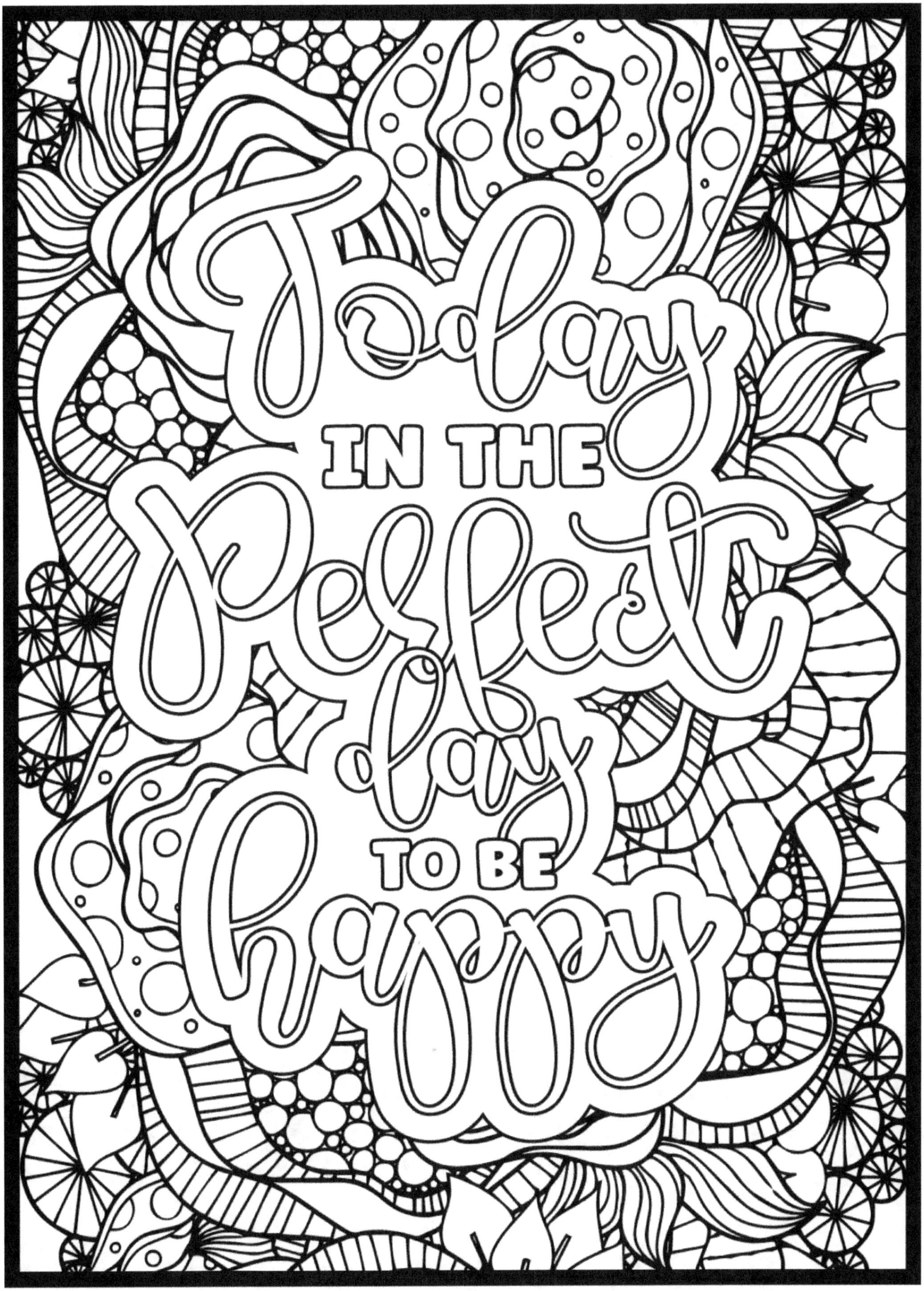
Today
IN THE
Perfect
day
TO BE
happy

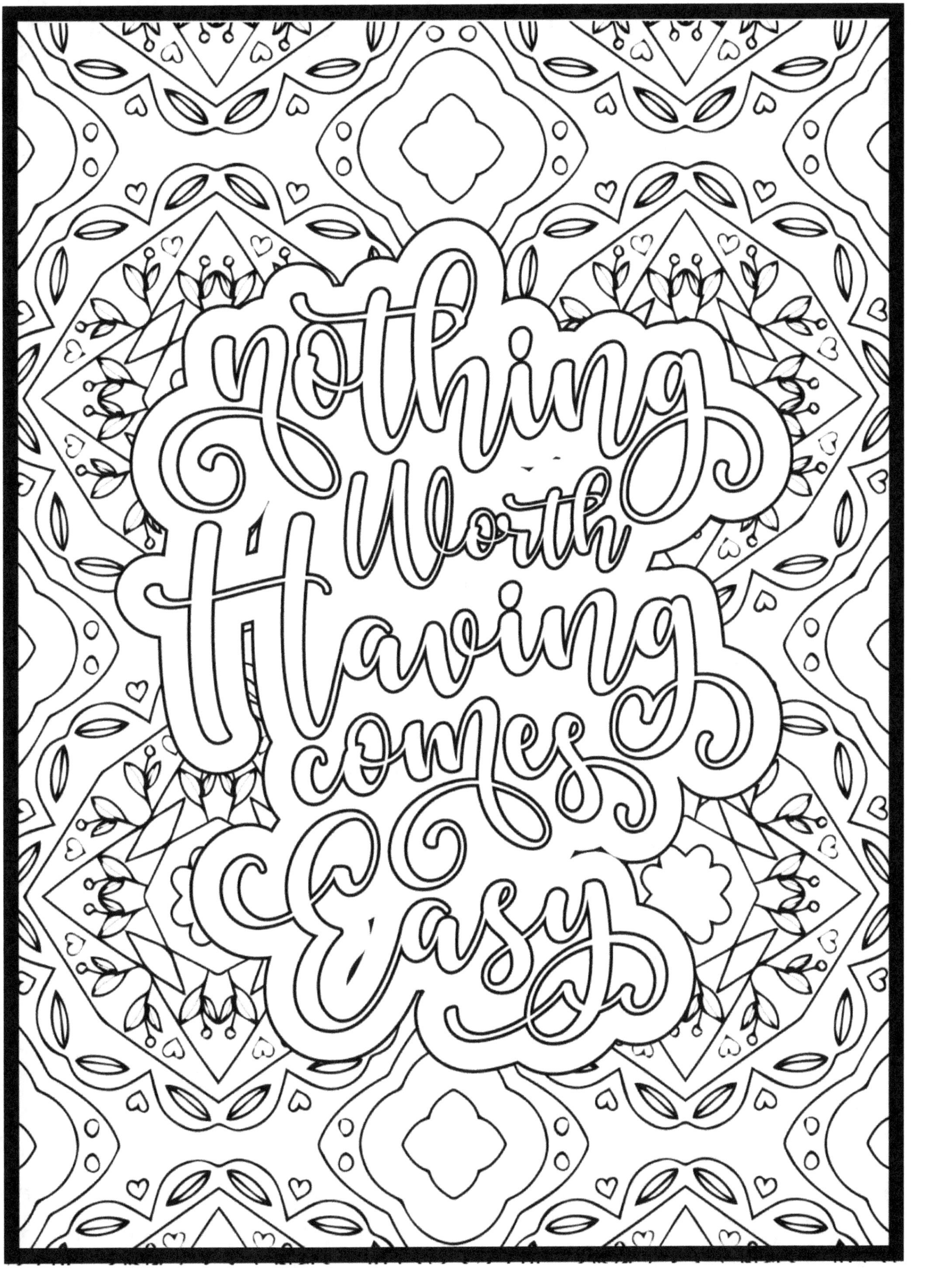
nothing Worth Having comes Easy

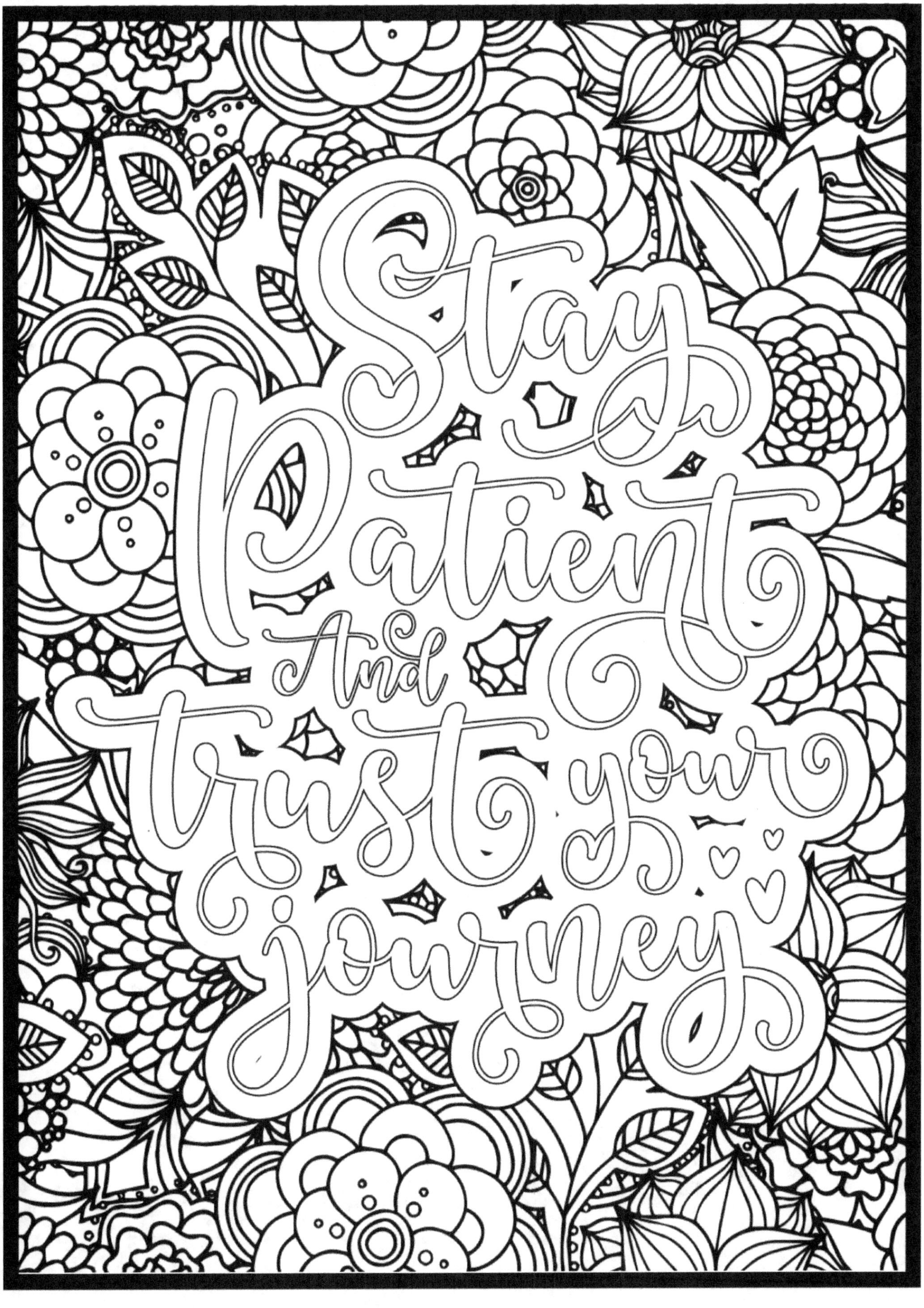
Stay
Patient
And
trust your
journey

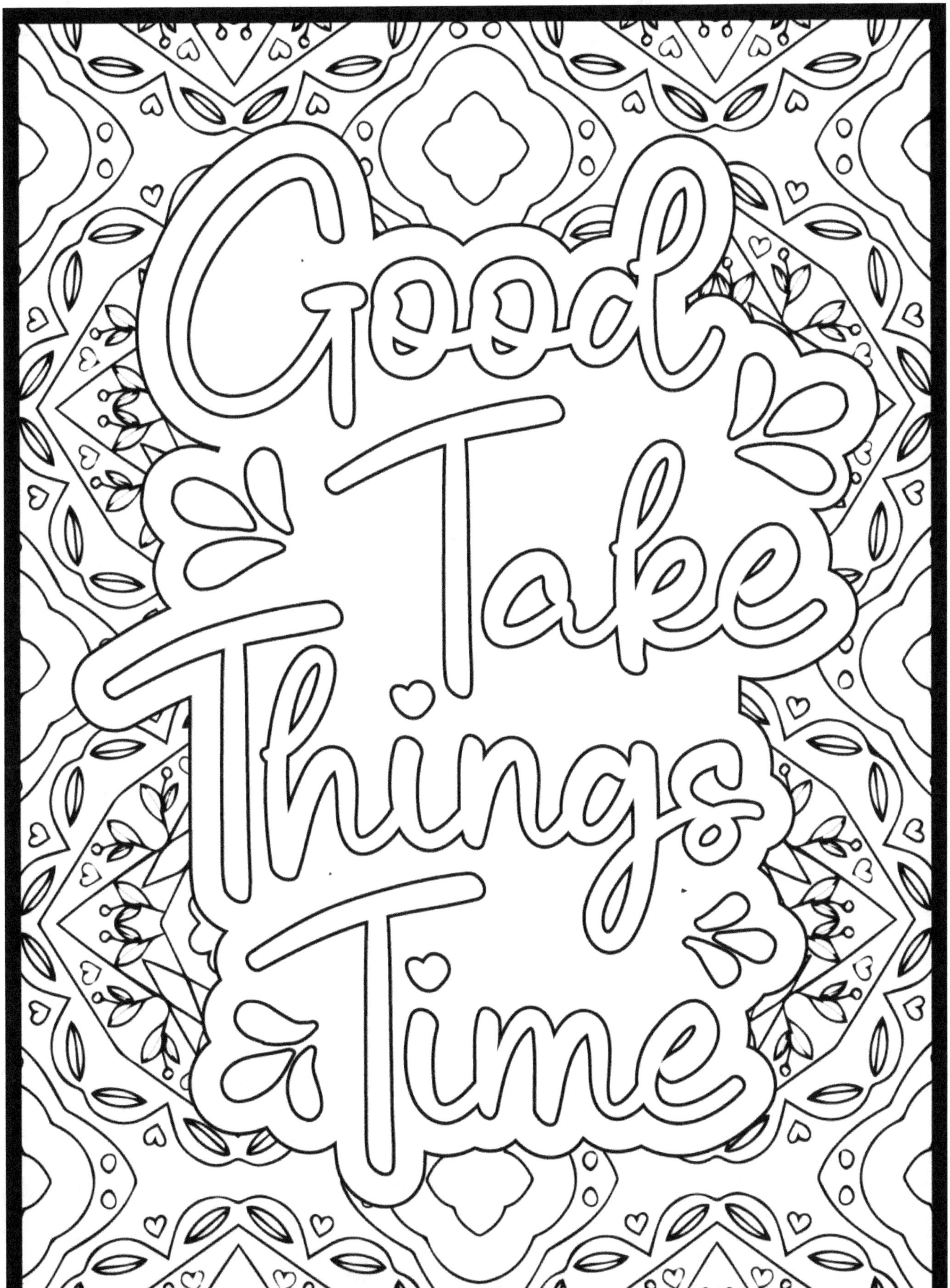
Good
Take
Things
Time

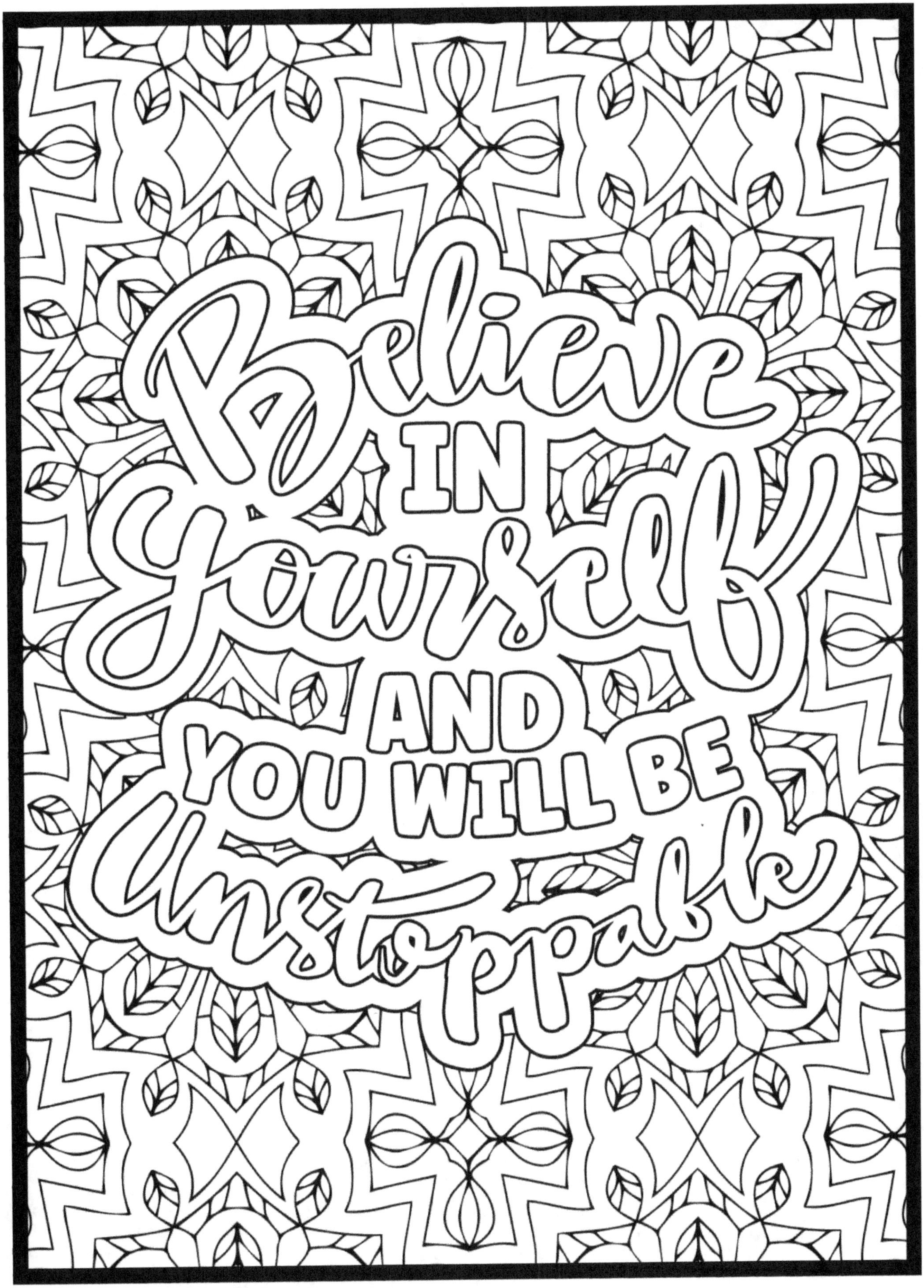
Believe
IN
Yourself
AND
YOU WILL BE
Unstoppable

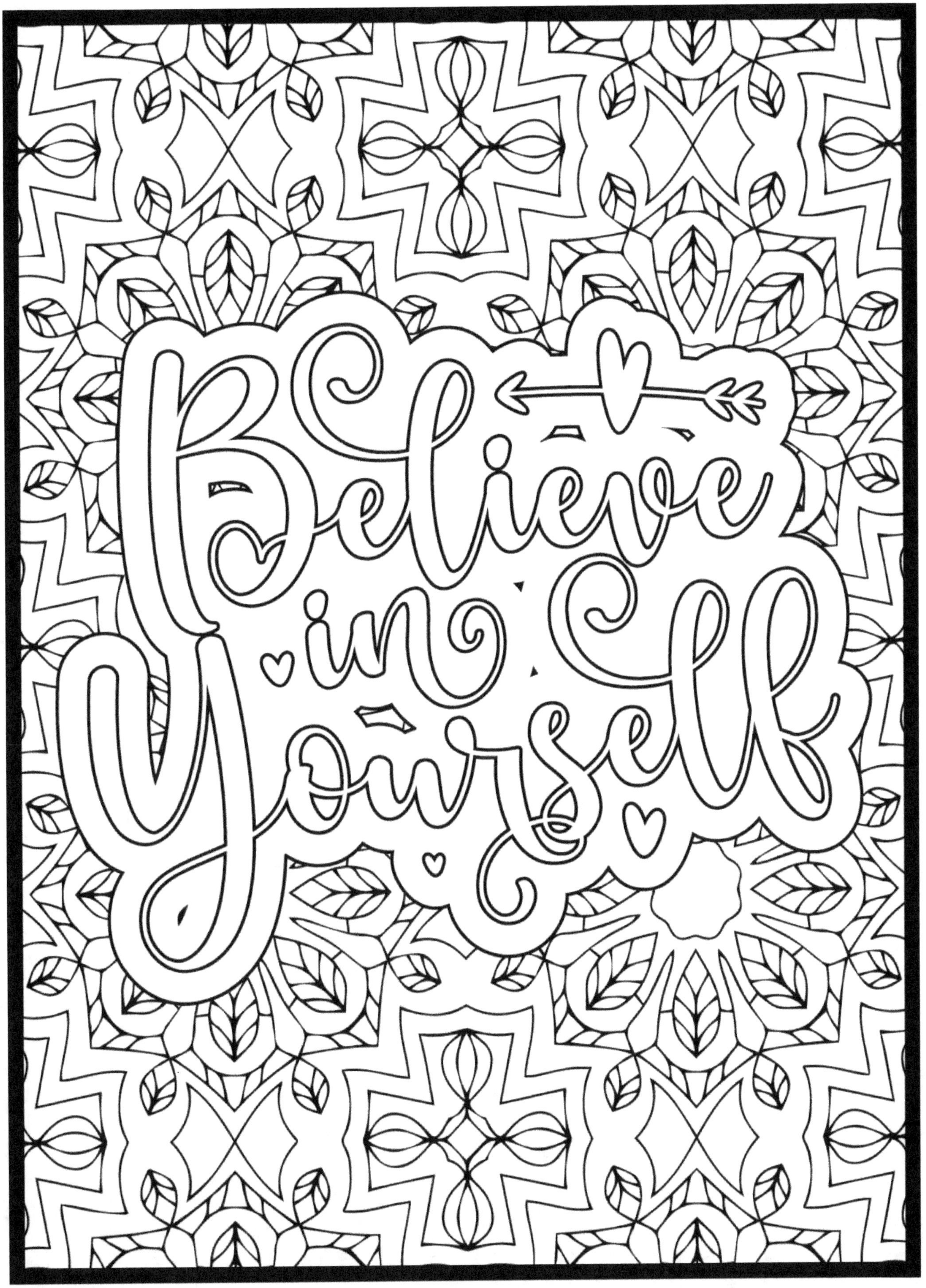
Believe in Yourself

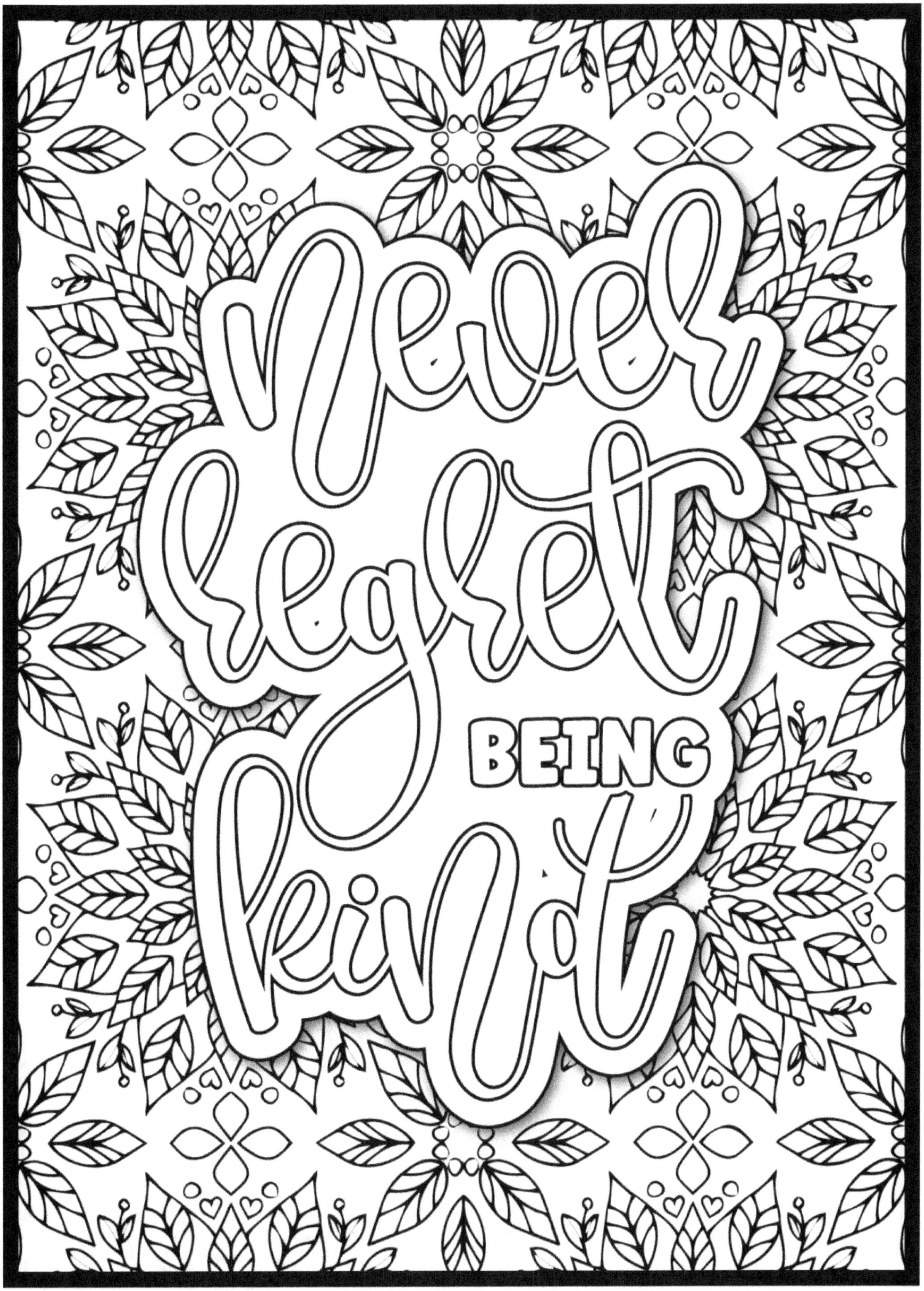
never regret
BEING
kind

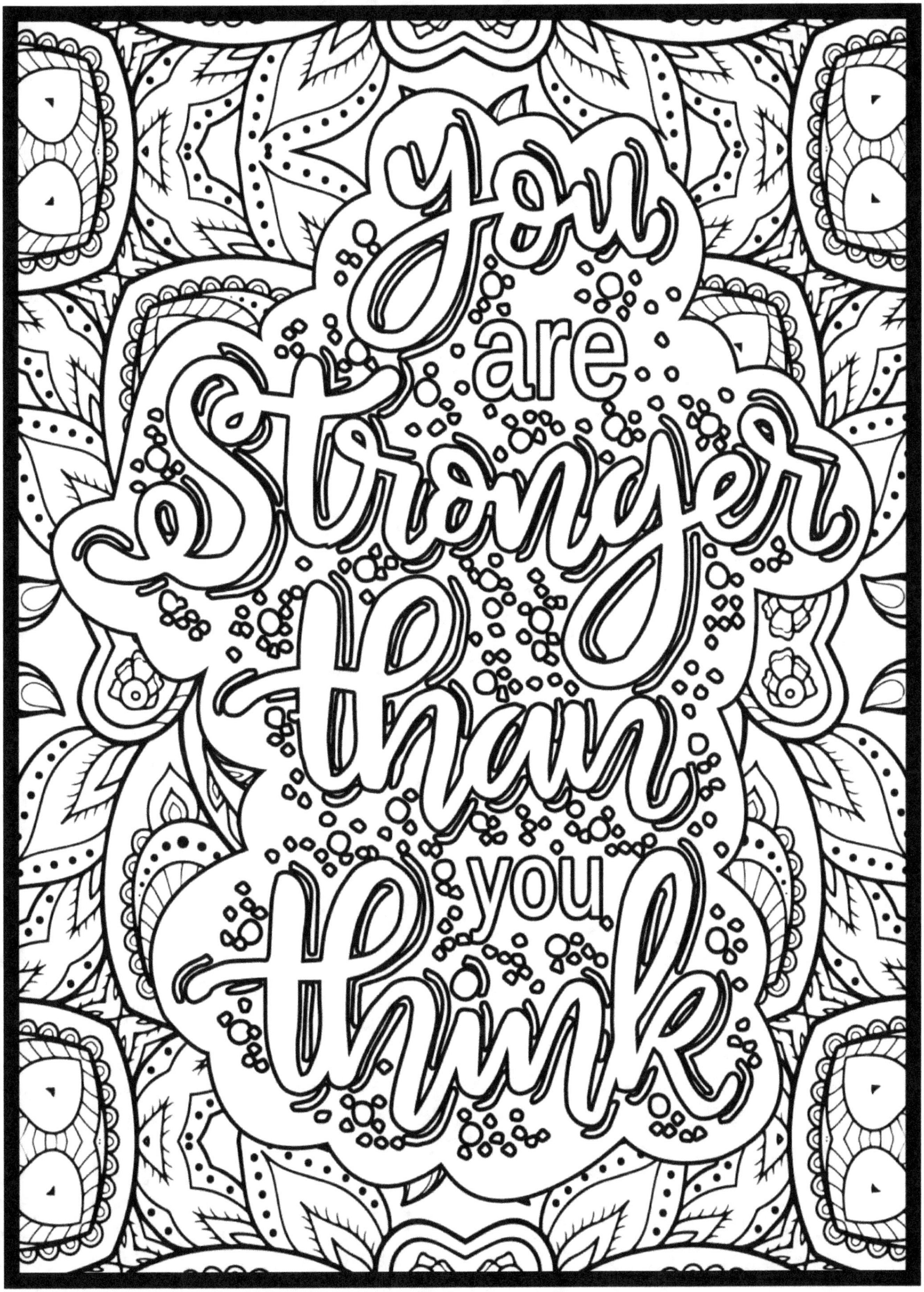
You are Stronger than you think

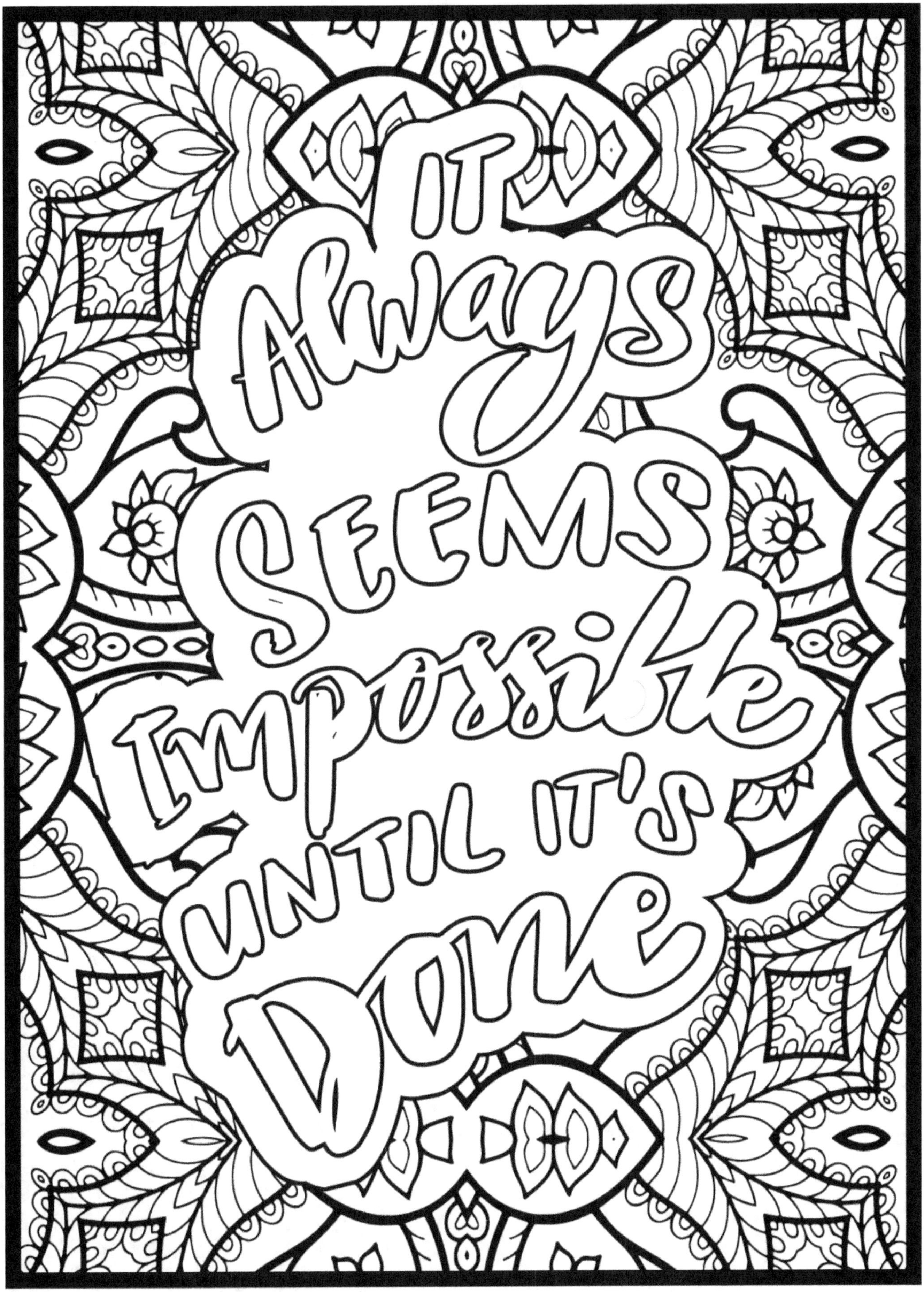
It Always Seems Impossible Until It's Done

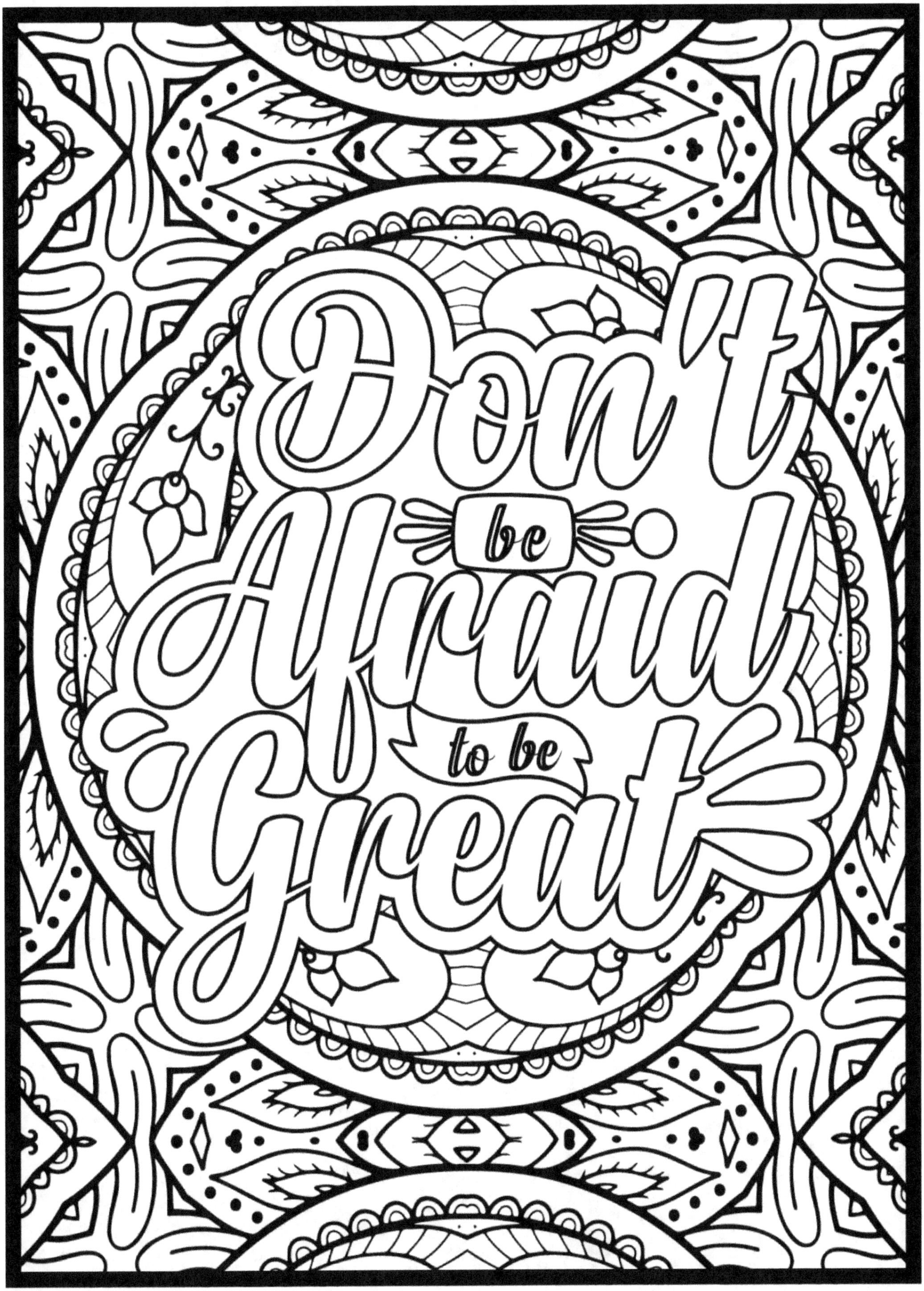
Don't
be
Afraid
to be
Great

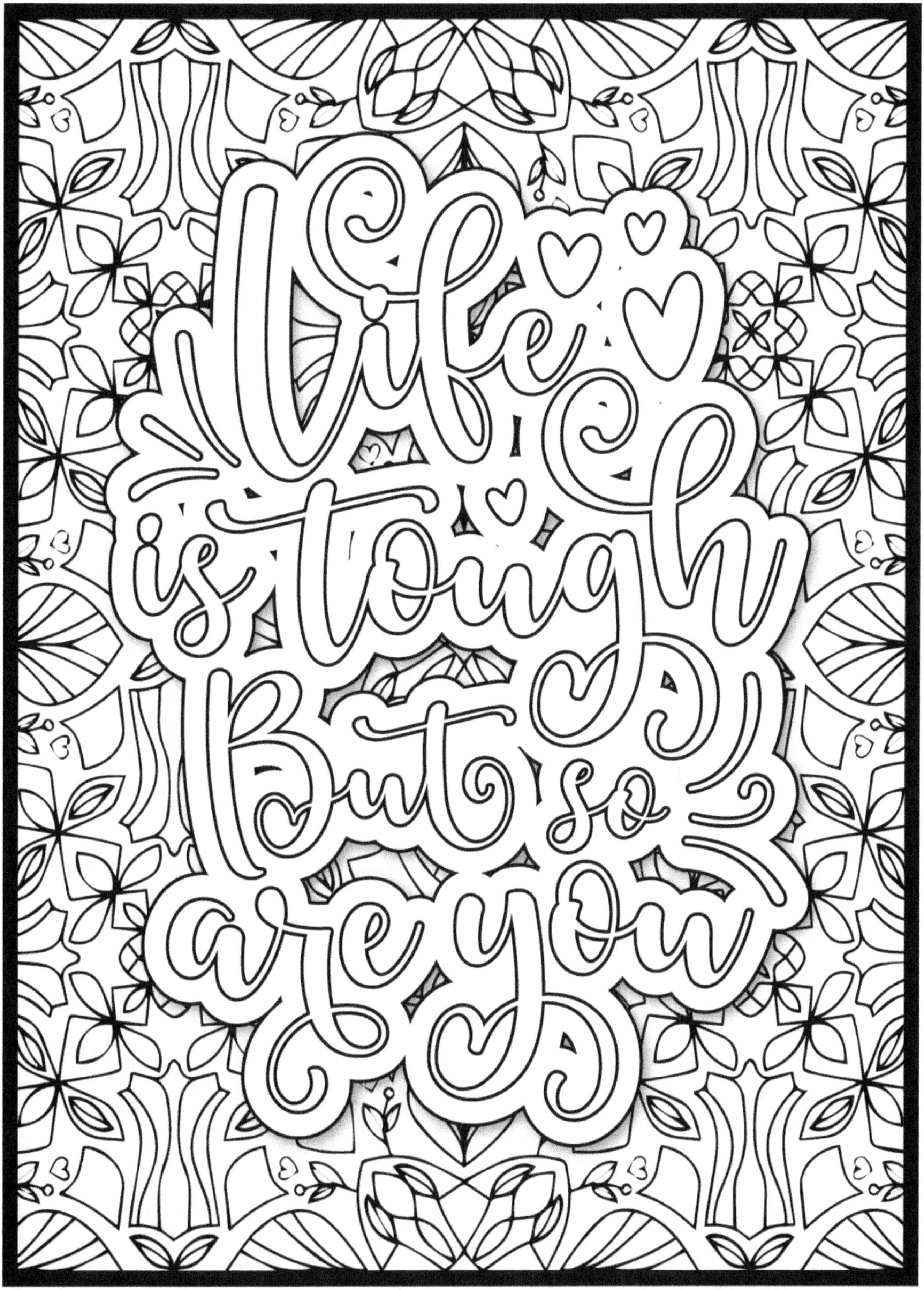
Life is tough
But so are you

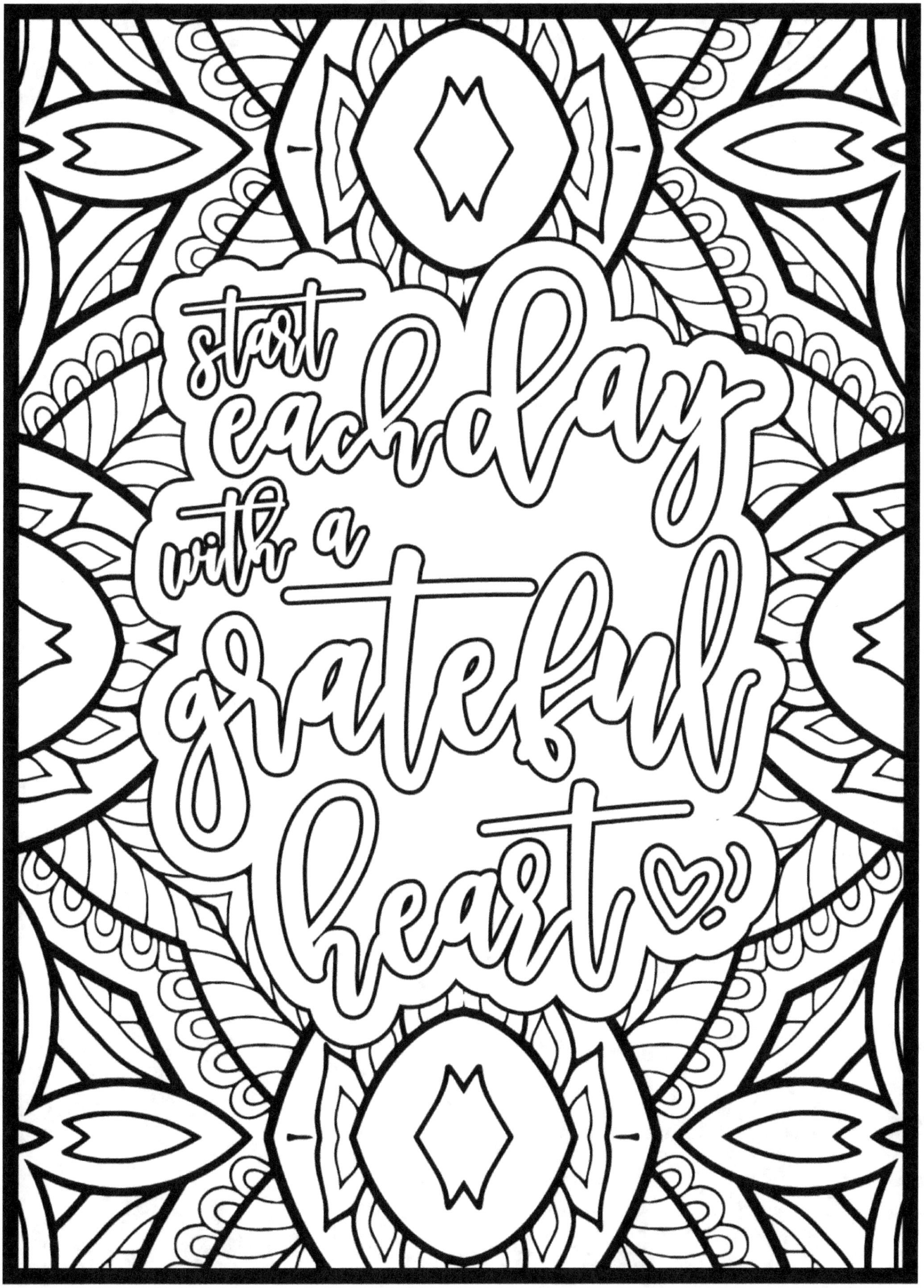
start each day with a grateful heart

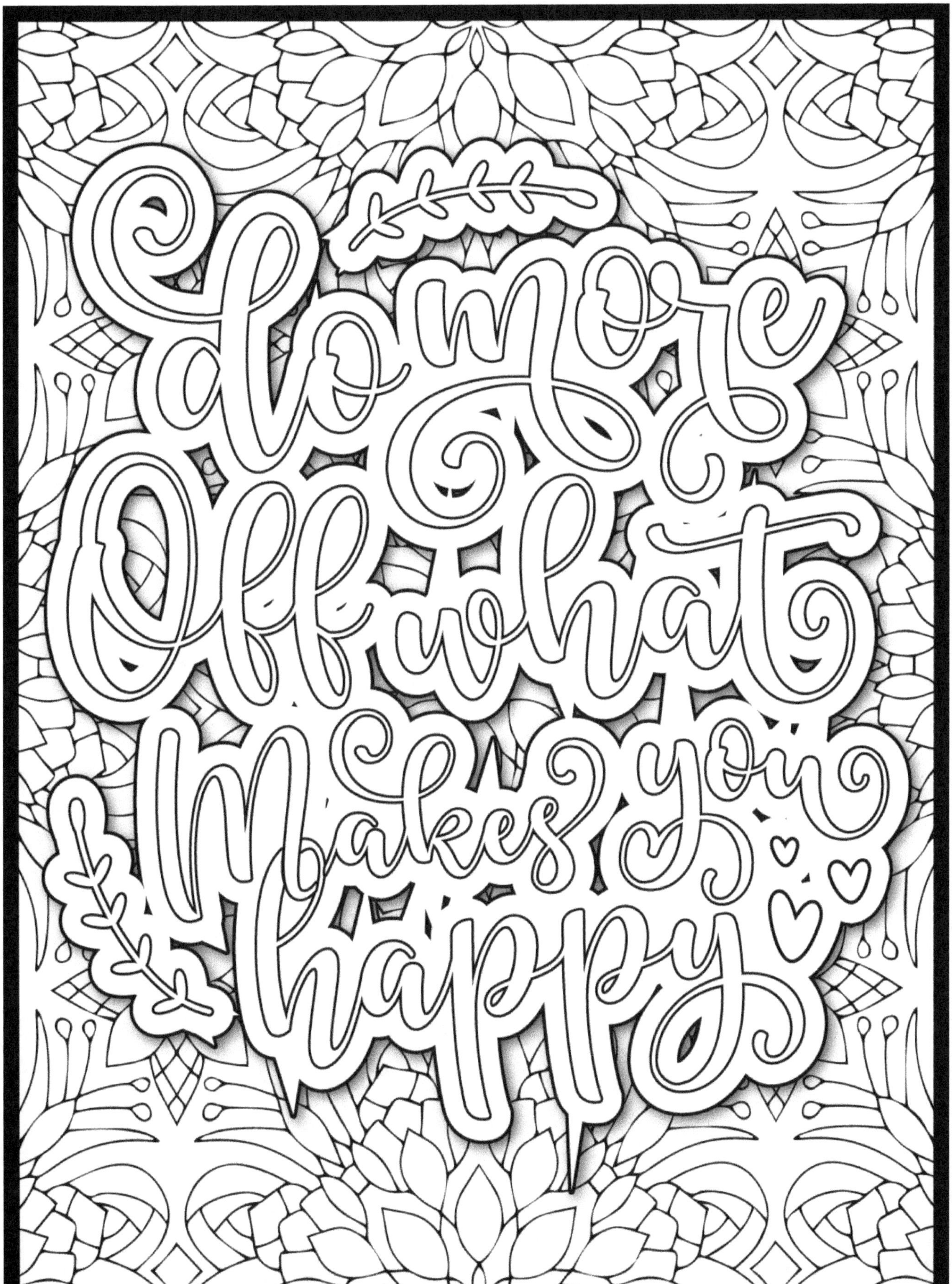
do more
Of what
Makes you
happy

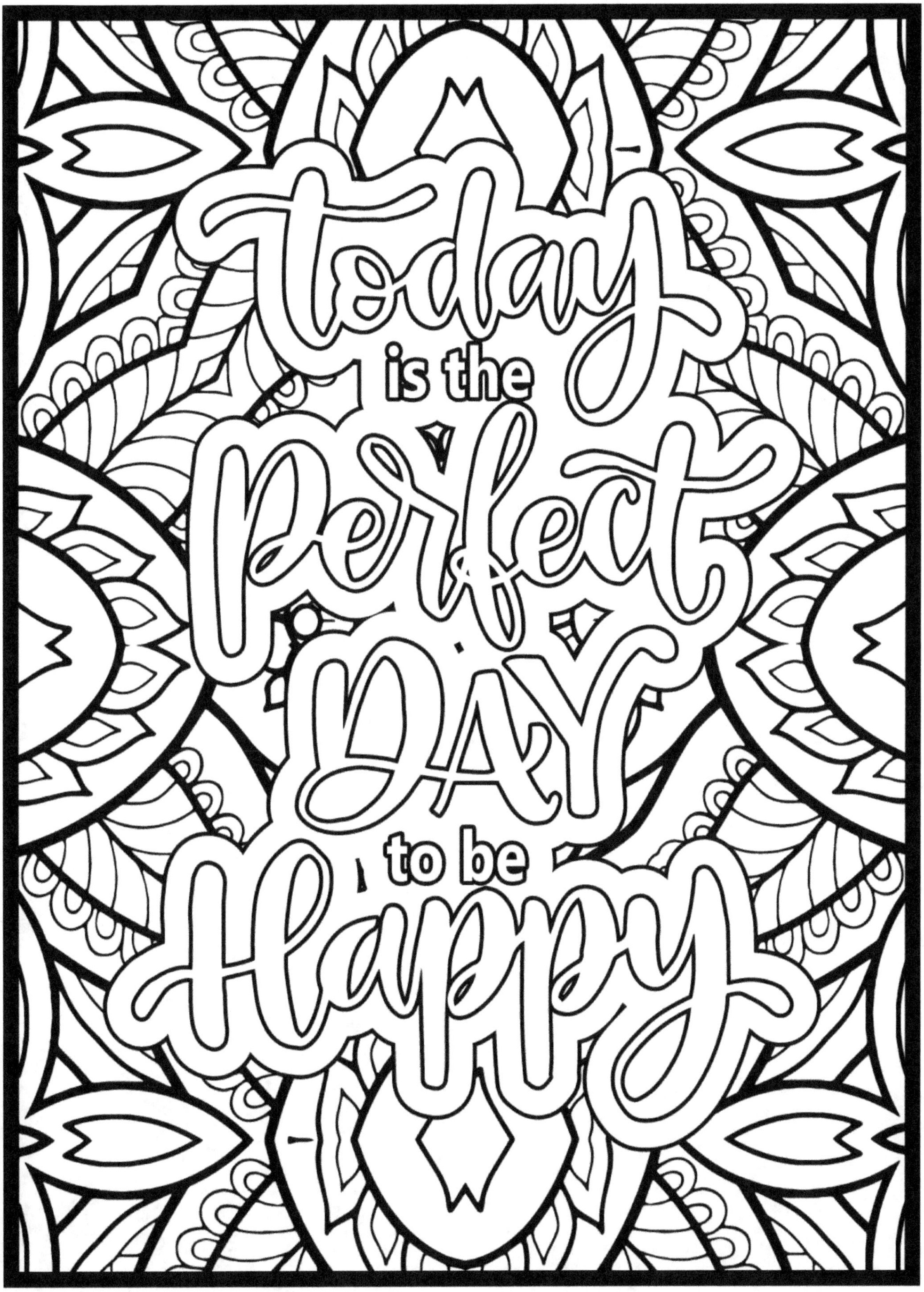
Today
is the
Perfect
DAY
to be
Happy

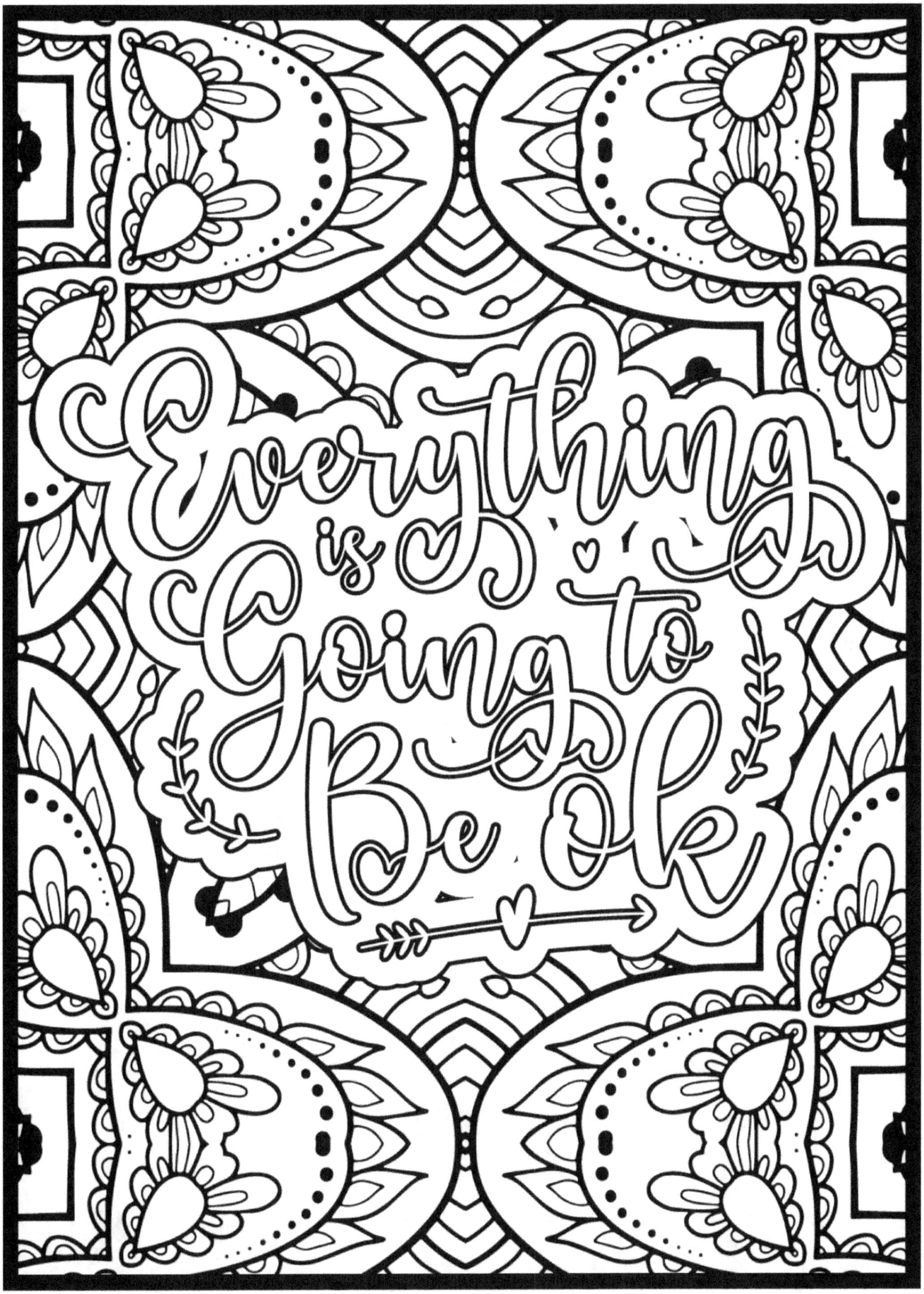
Everything
is
Going to
Be Ok

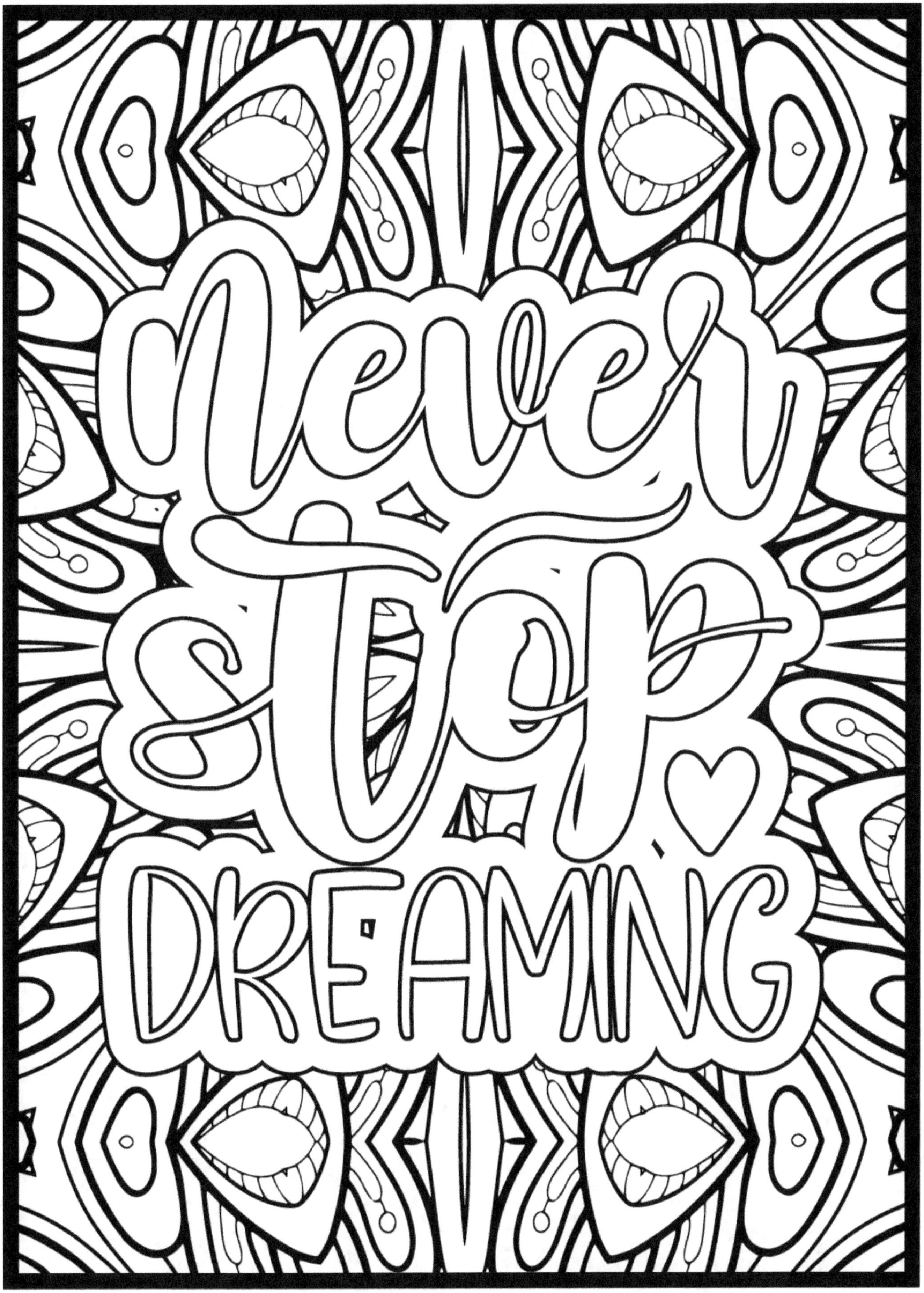
never
stop
DREAMING

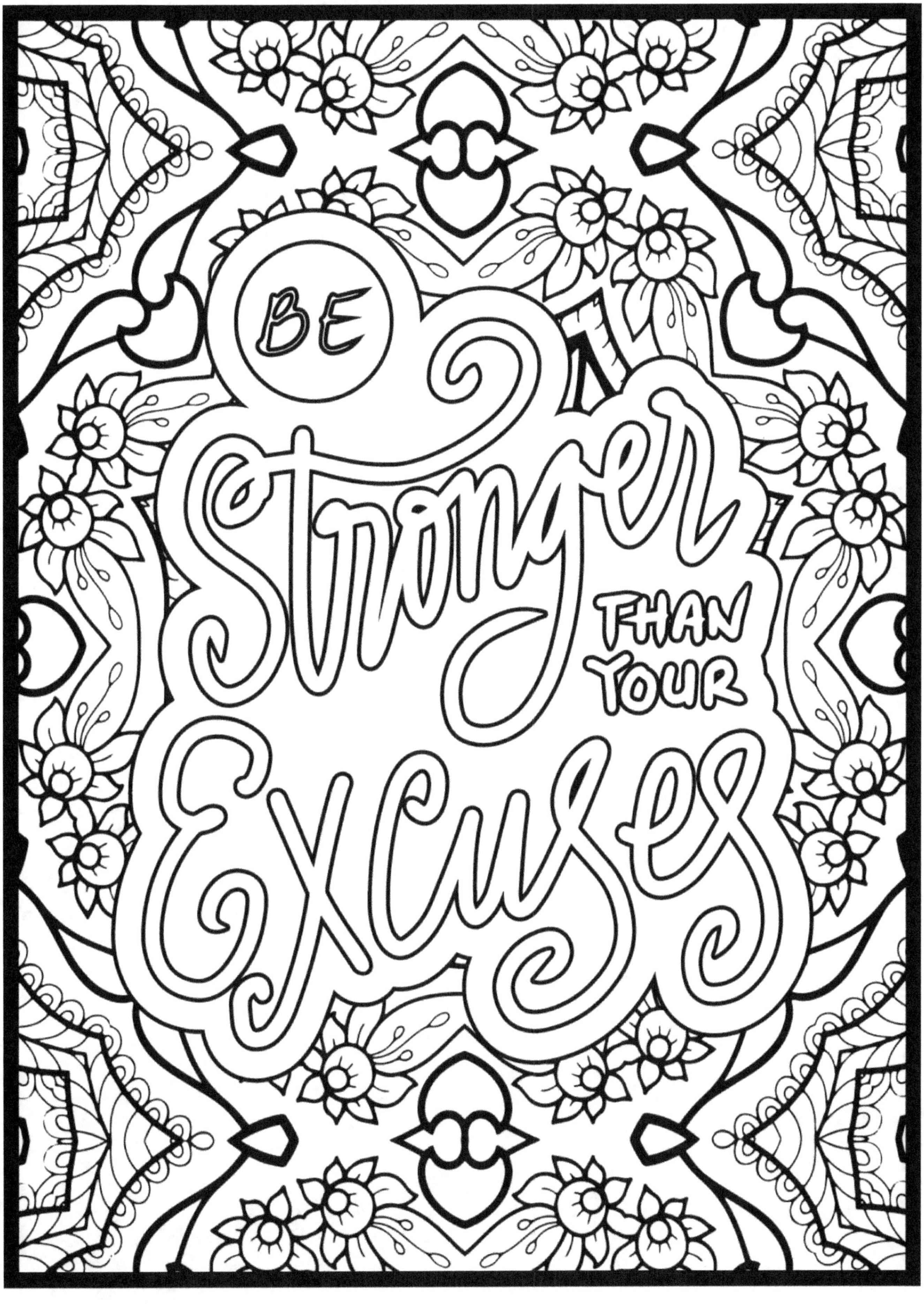
BE
Stronger
THAN YOUR
Excuses

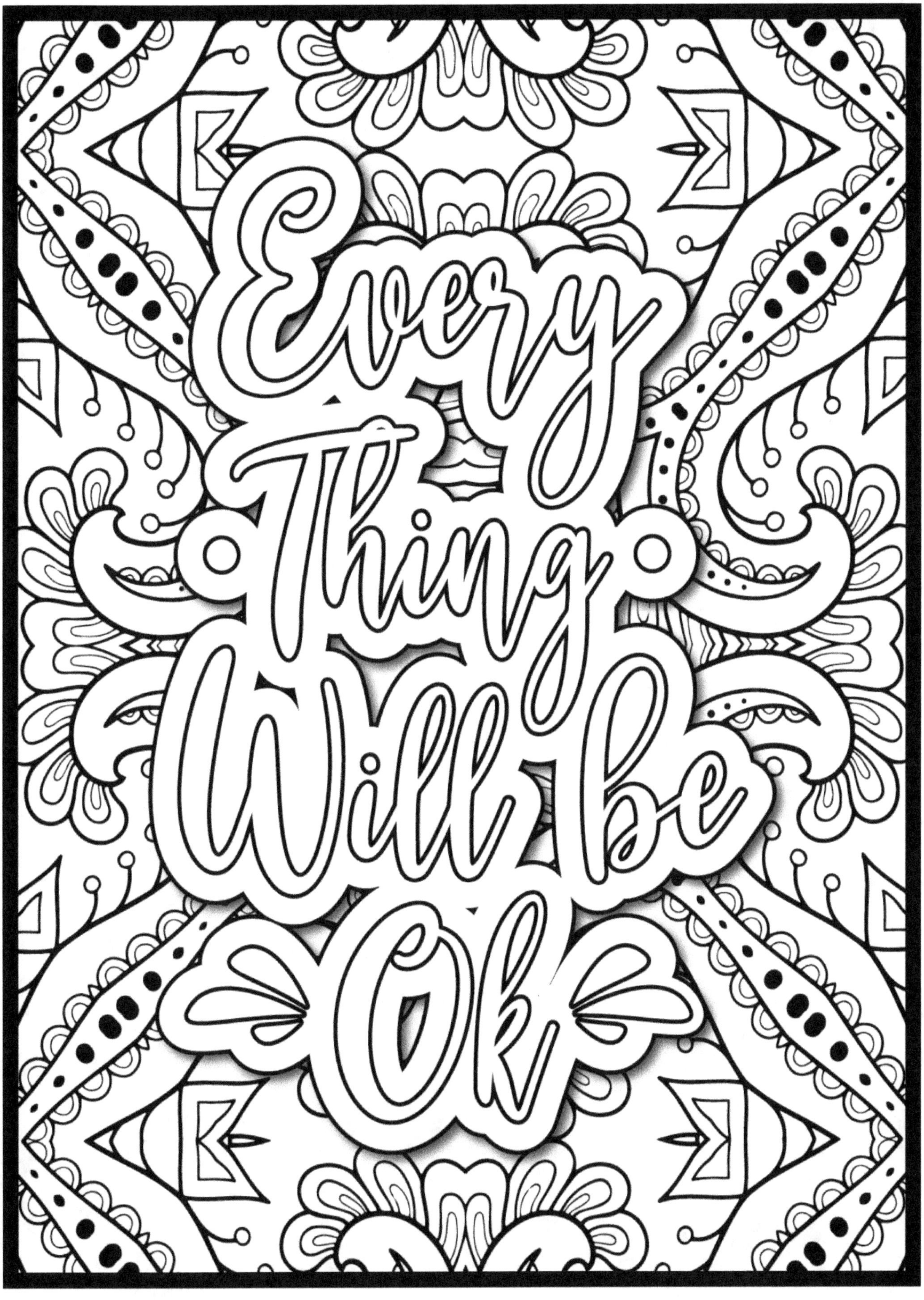
Every
Thing
Will be
Ok

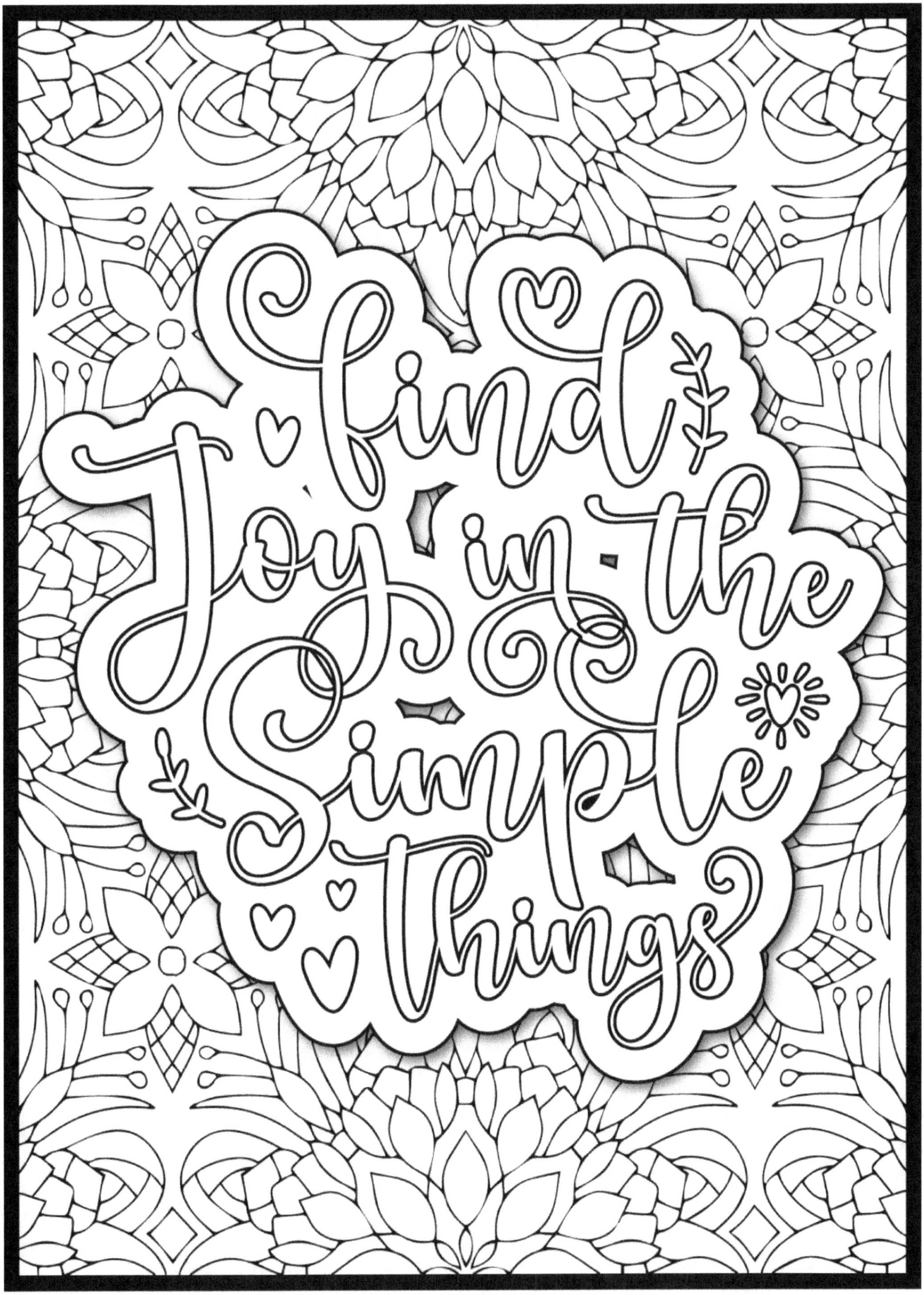
find Joy in the Simple things

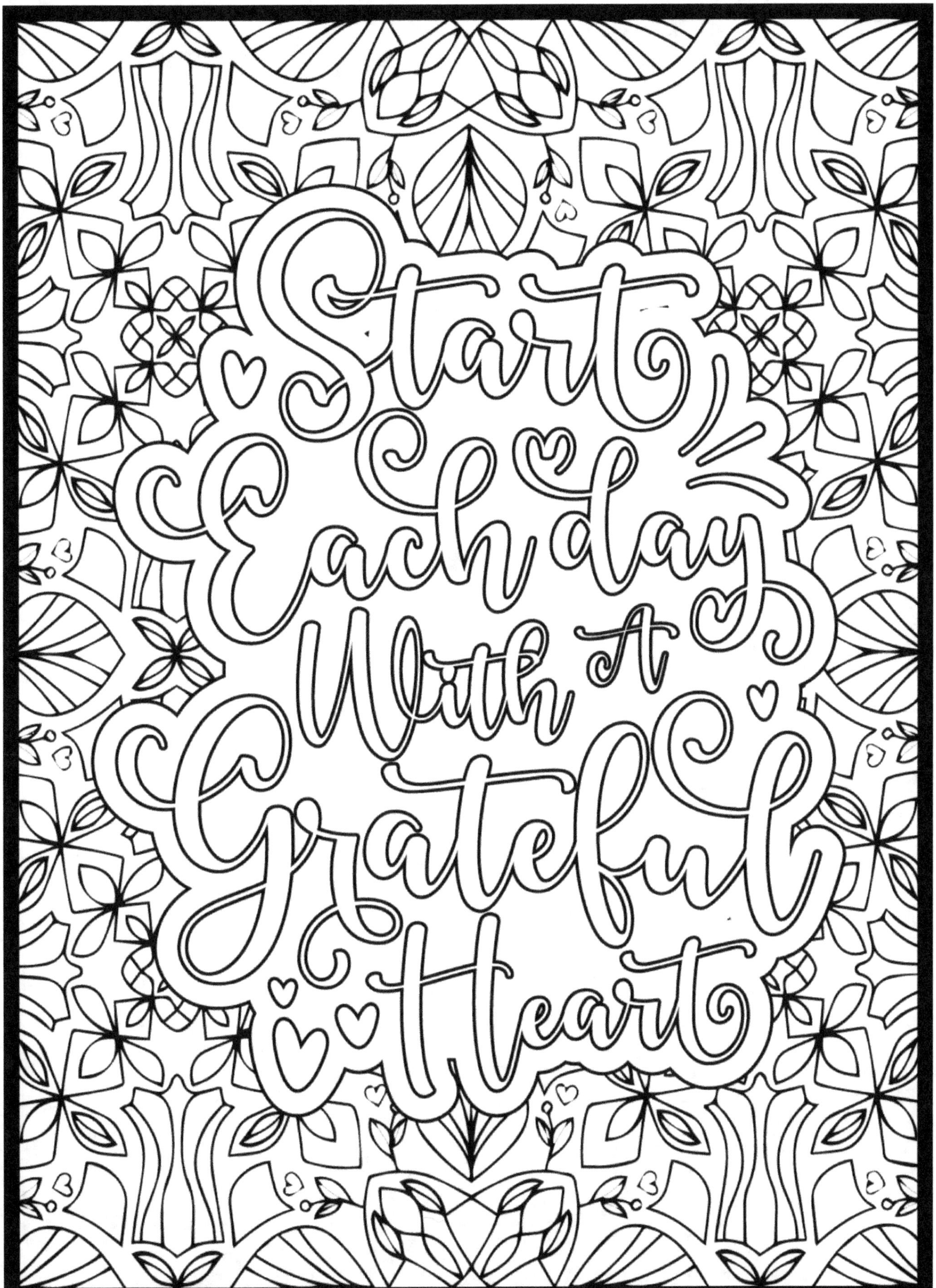
Start Each day With A Grateful Heart

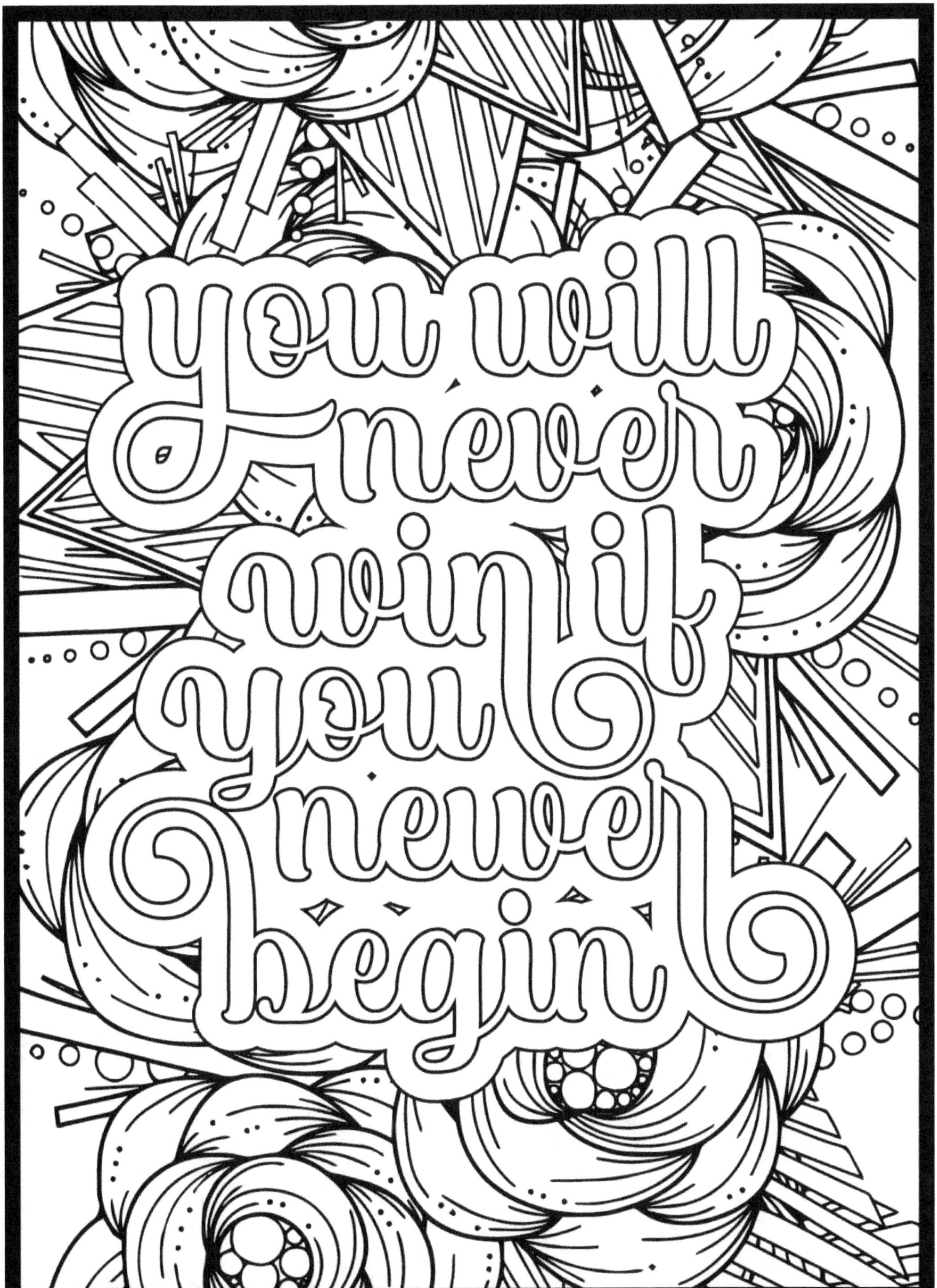
you will never win if you never begin

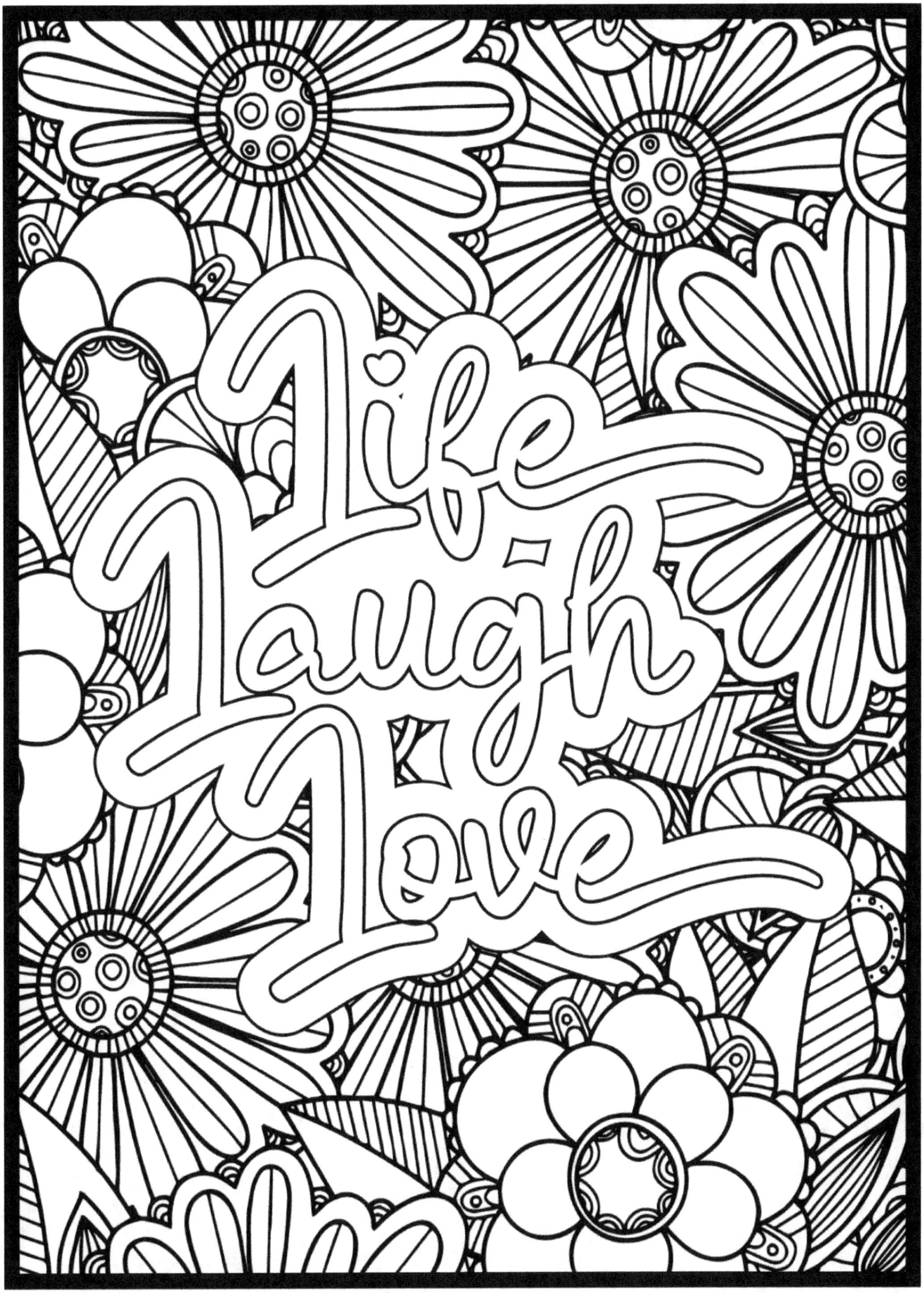
Life
Laugh
Love

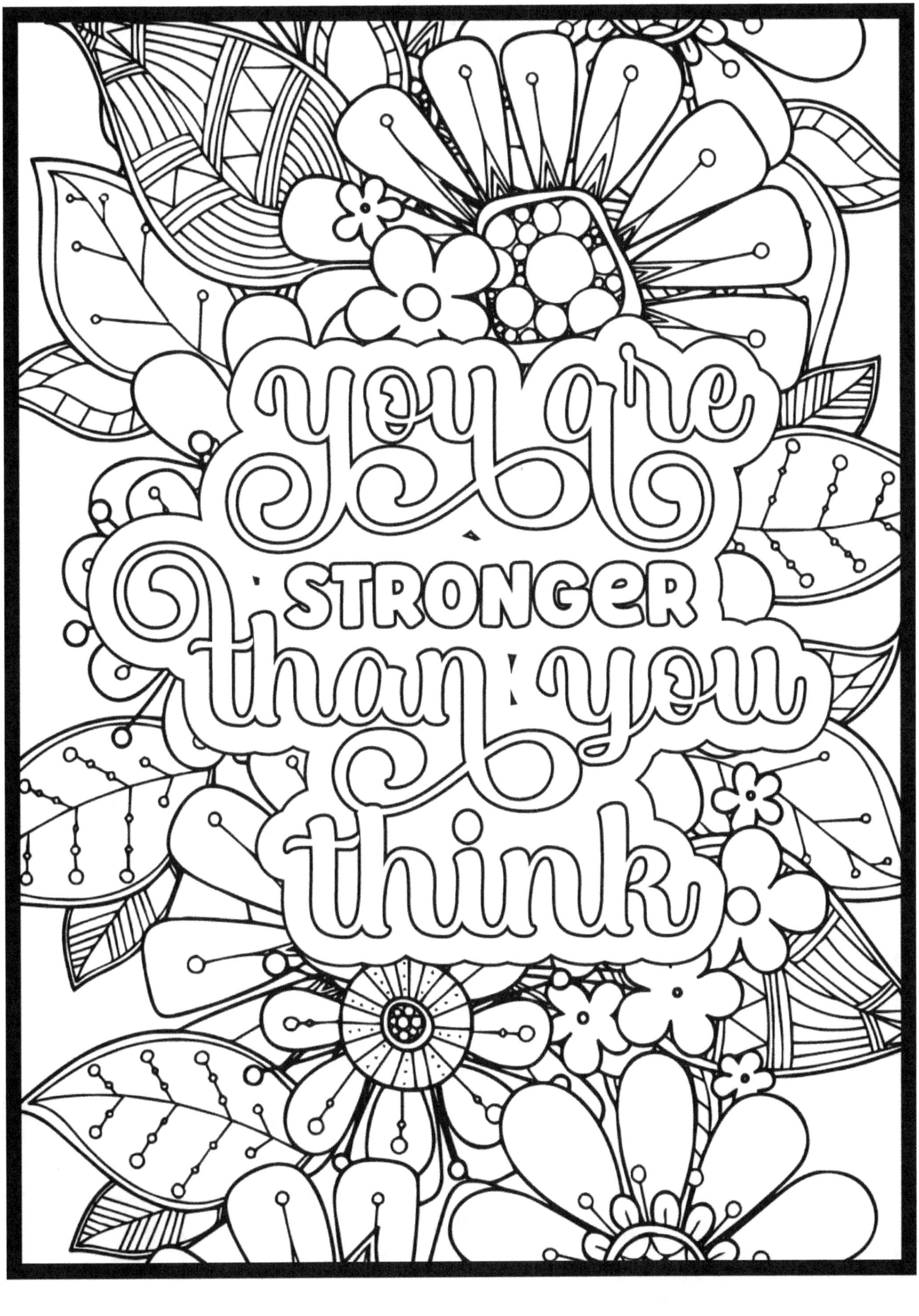
you are
STRONGER
than you
think

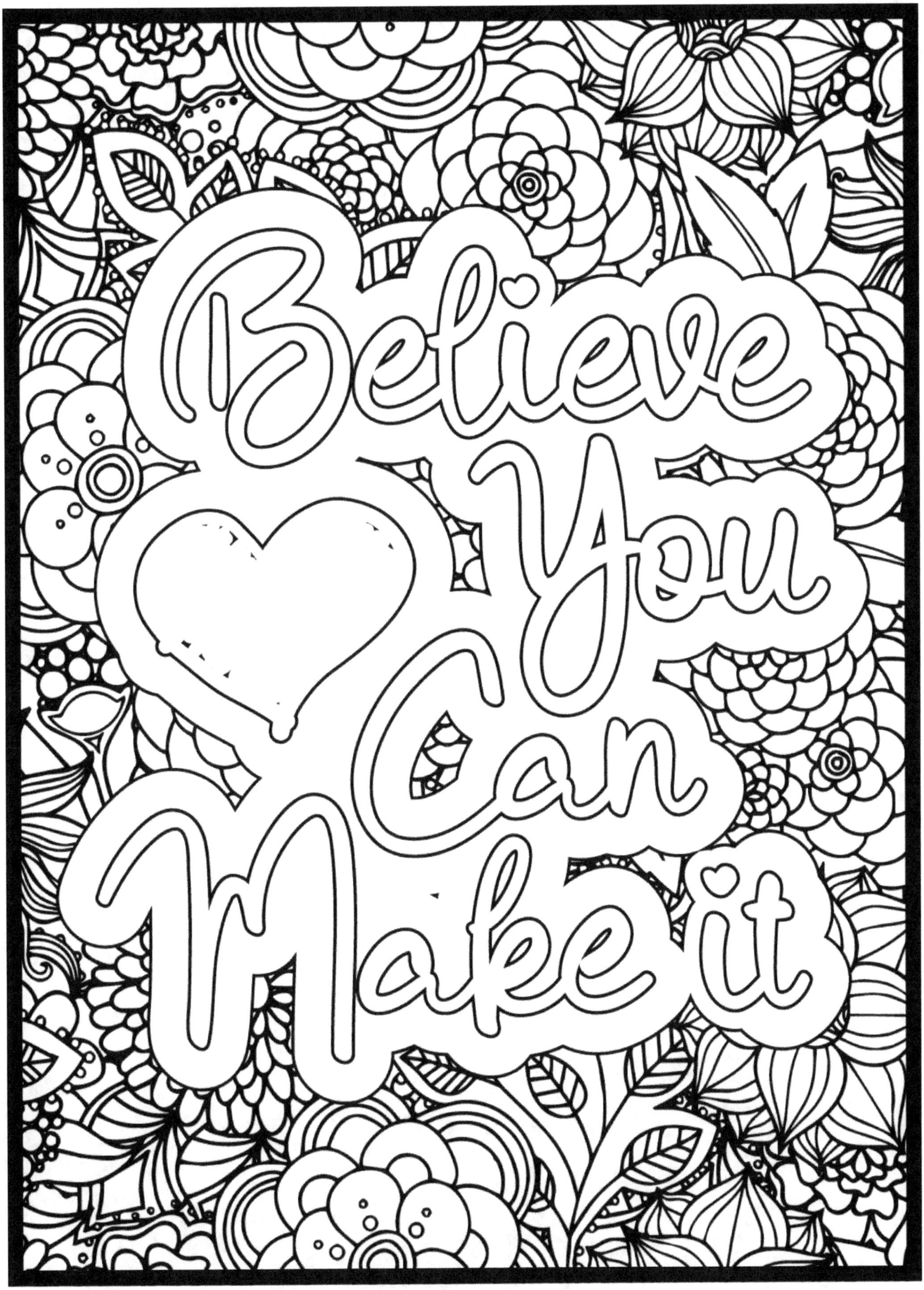
Believe You Can Make it

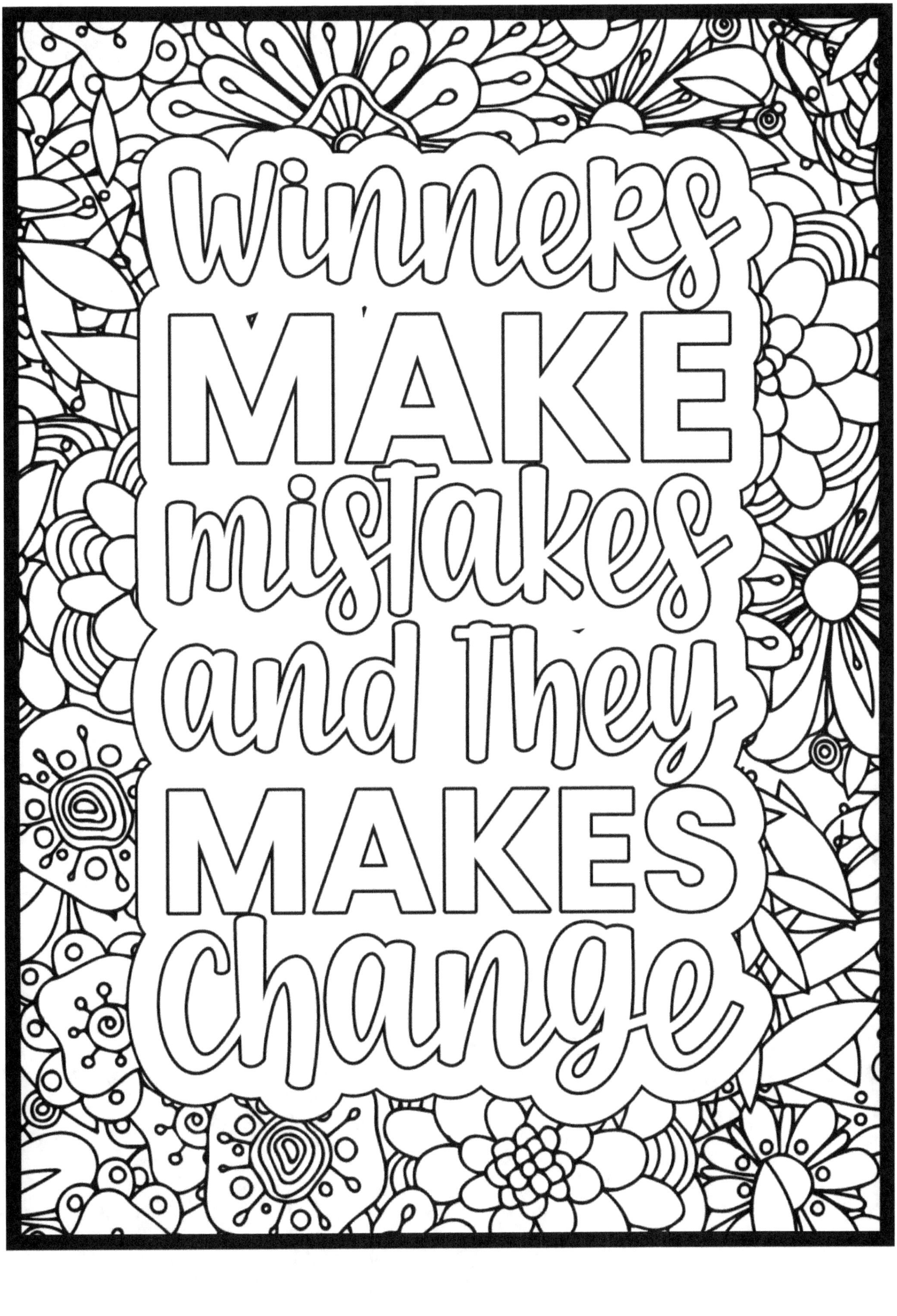
Winners
MAKE
mistakes
and They
MAKES
Change

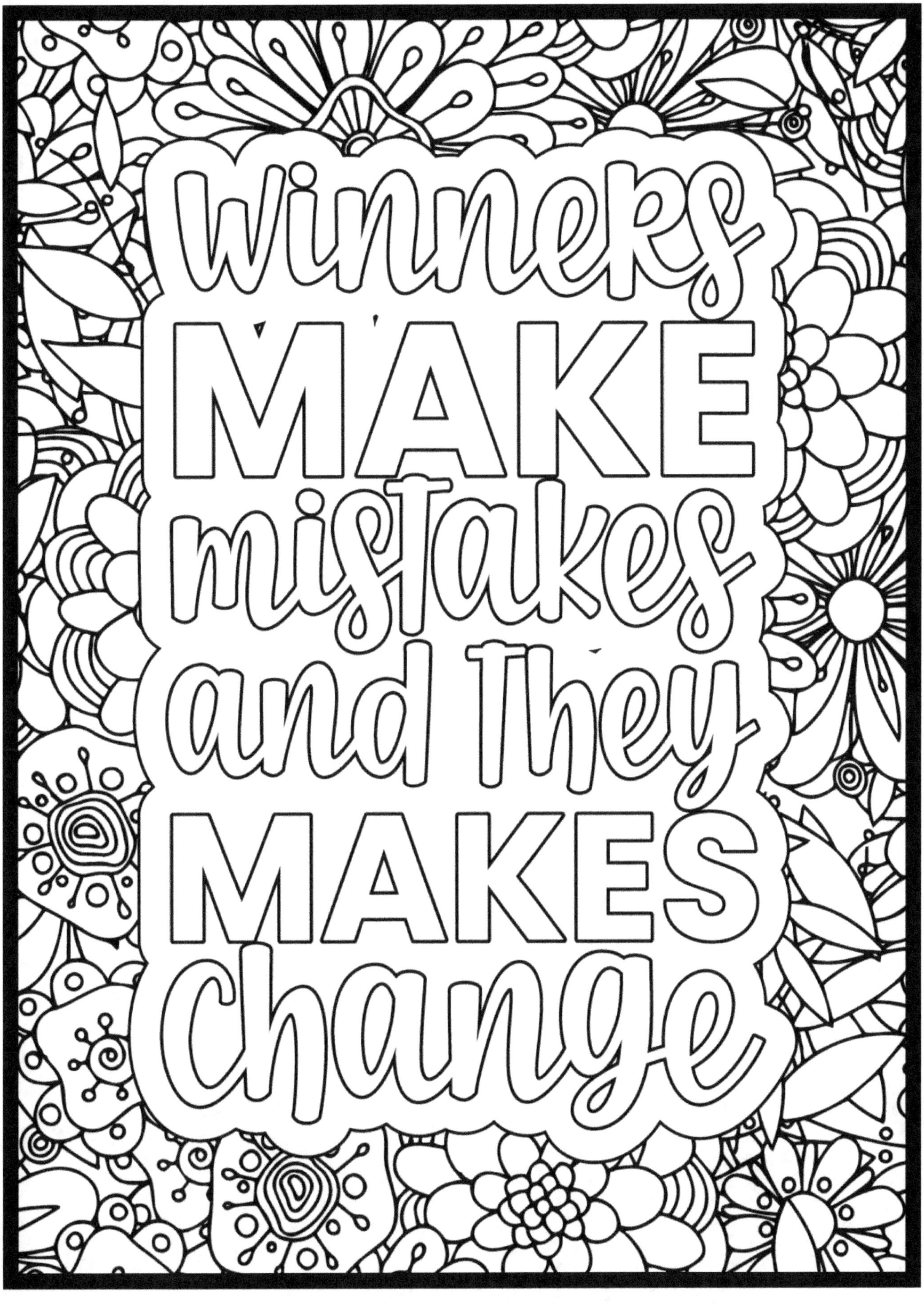
Winners
MAKE
mistakes
and They
MAKES
Change

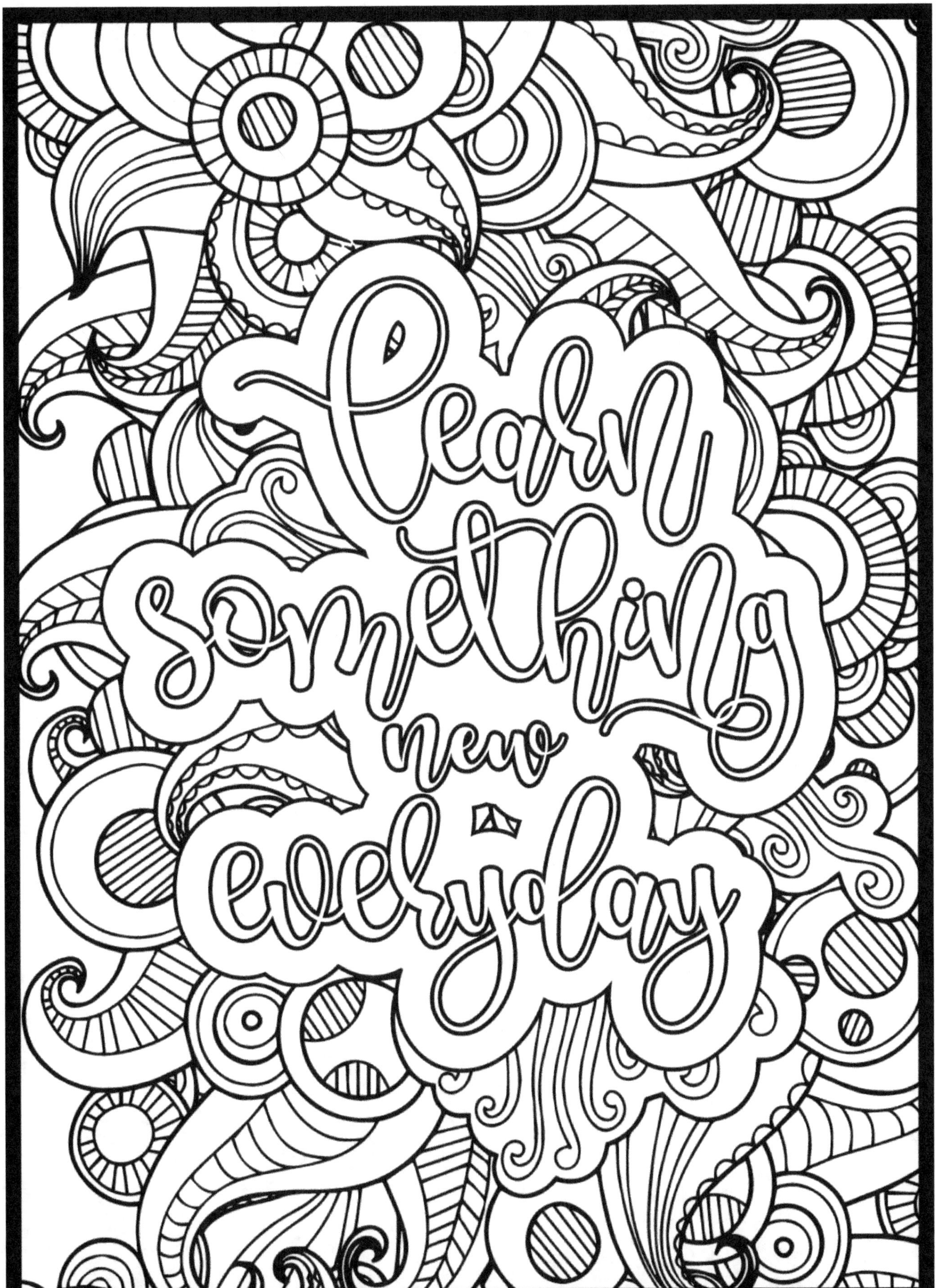
Learn something new everyday

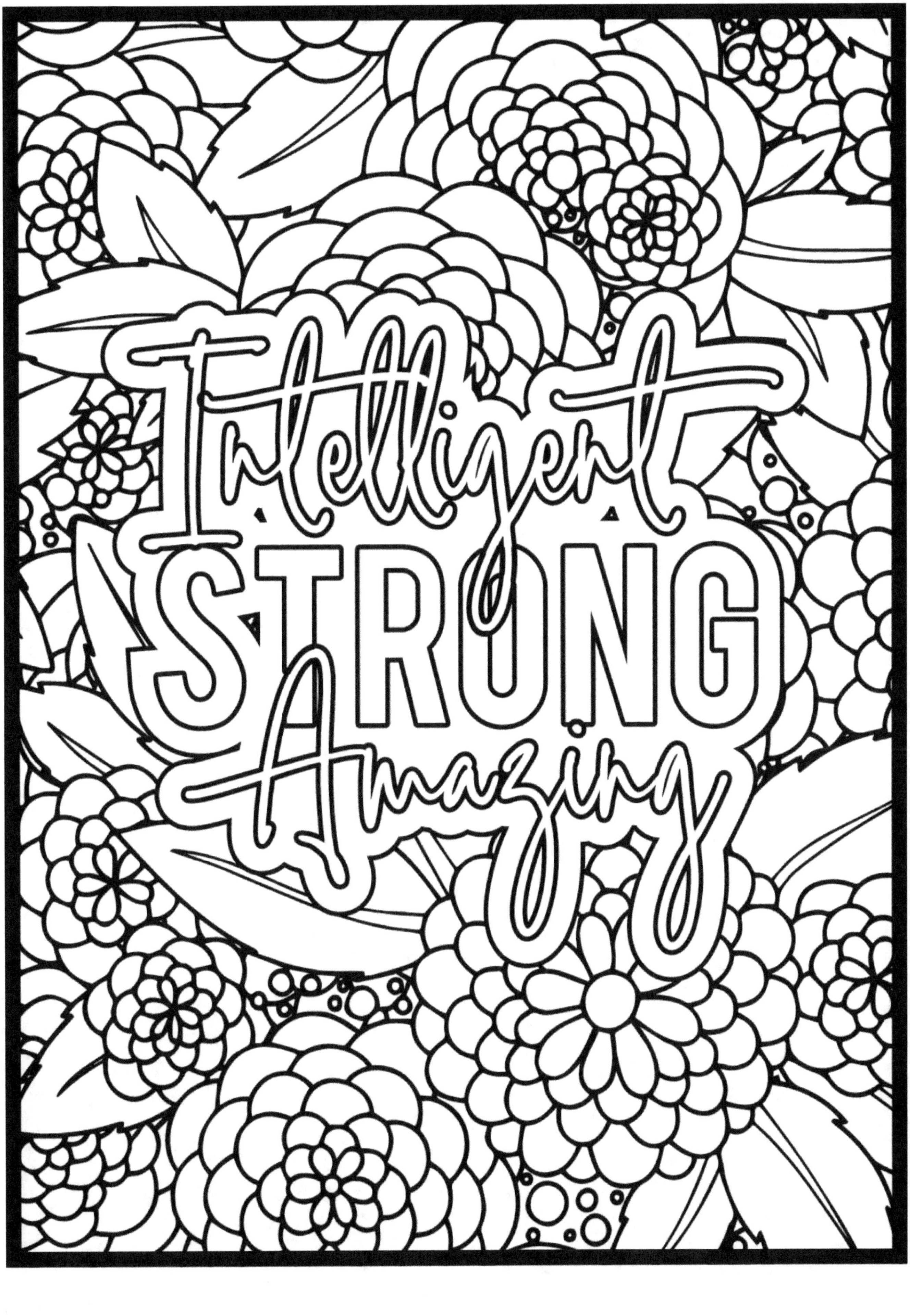
Intelligent
STRONG
Amazing

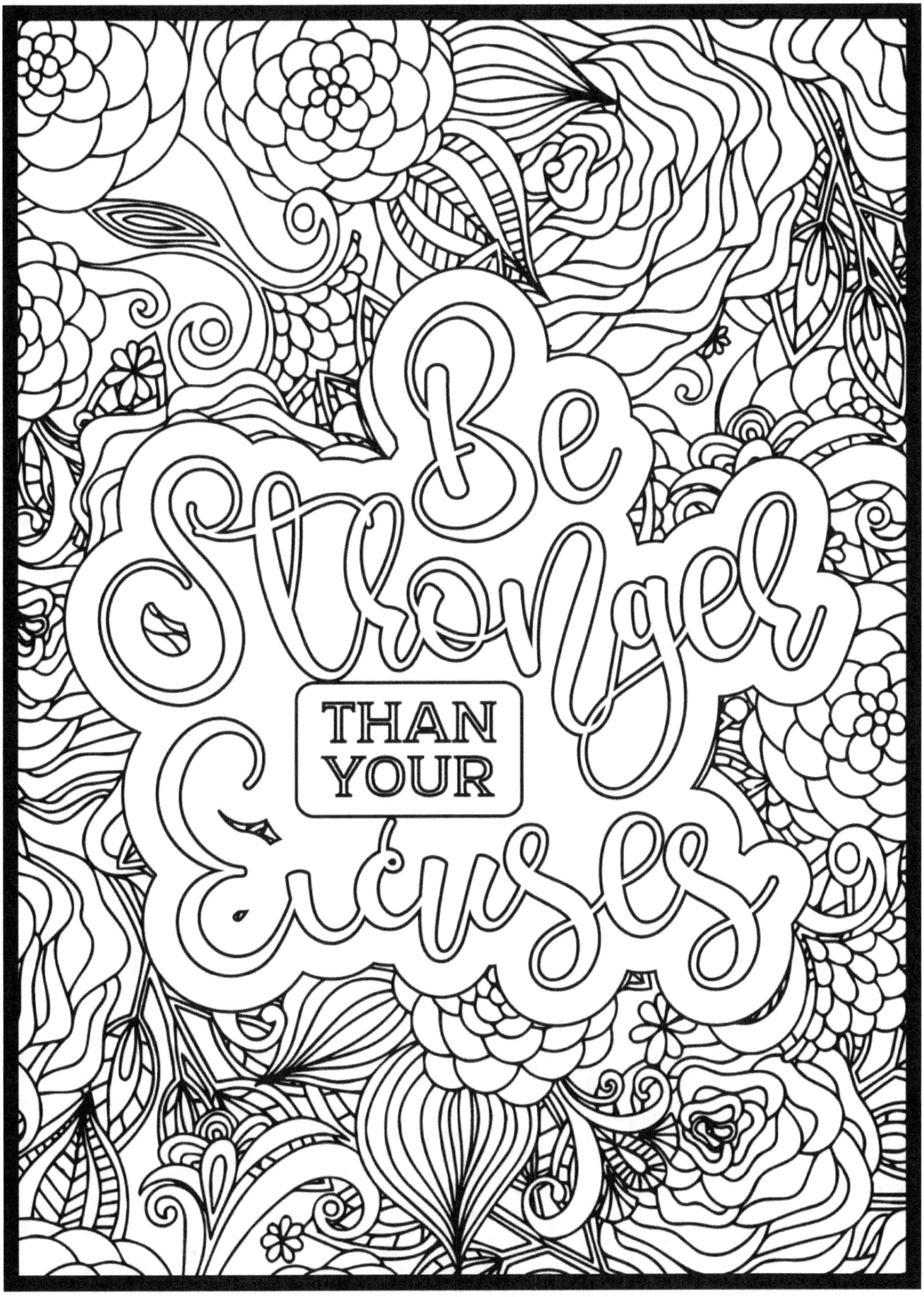
Be Stronger
THAN YOUR
Excuses

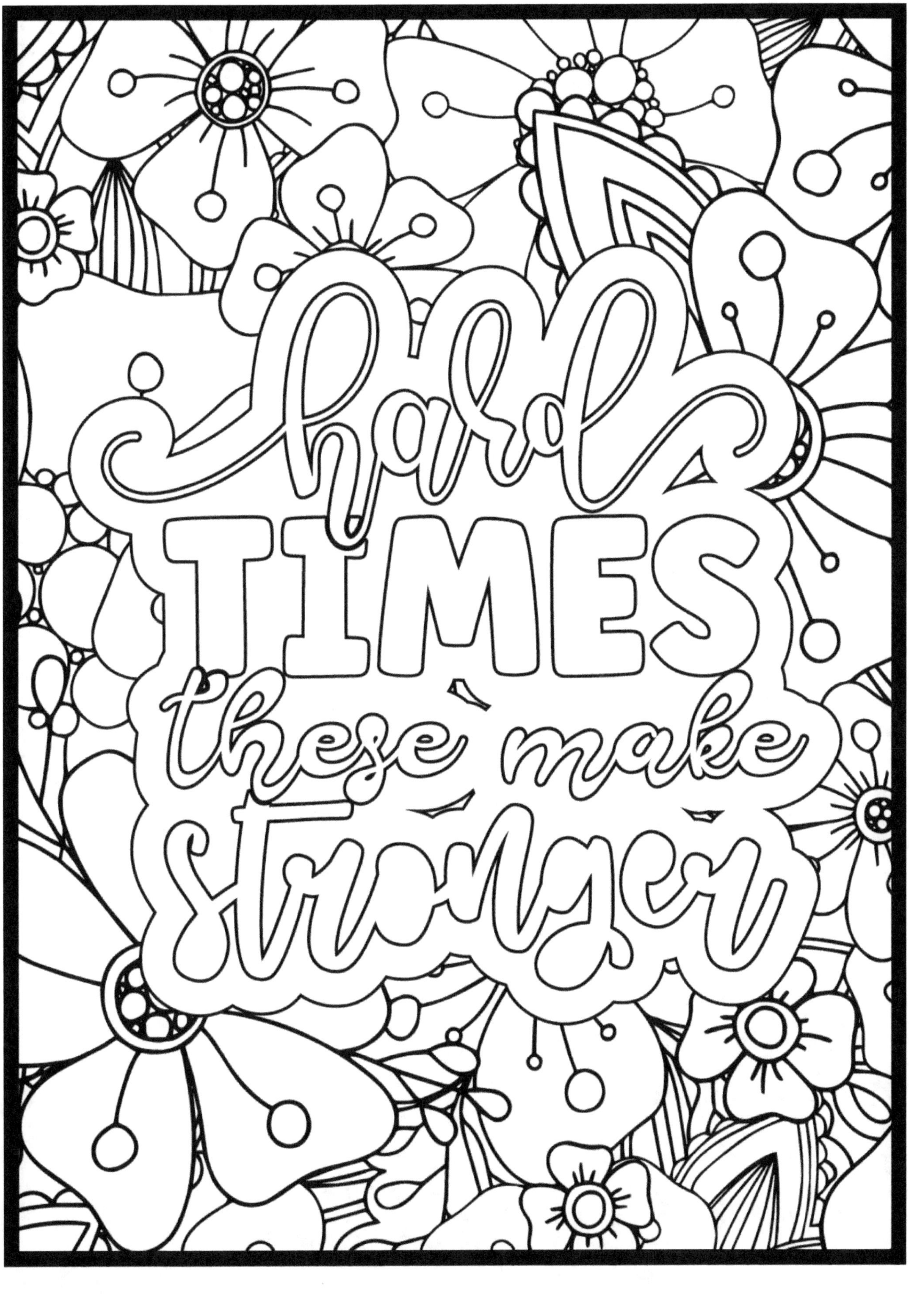
hard
TIMES
these make
stronger

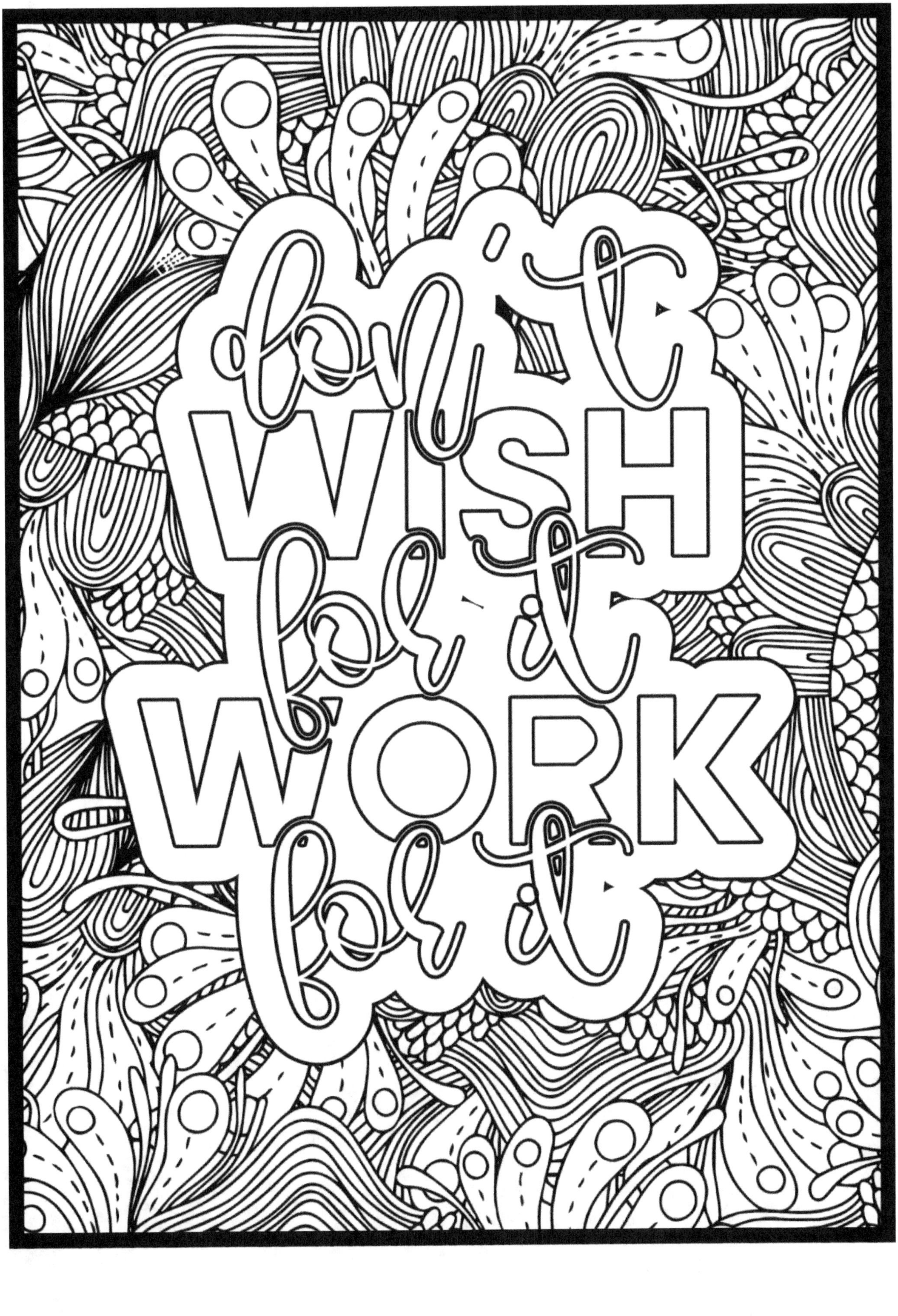
don't
WISH
for it
WORK
for it

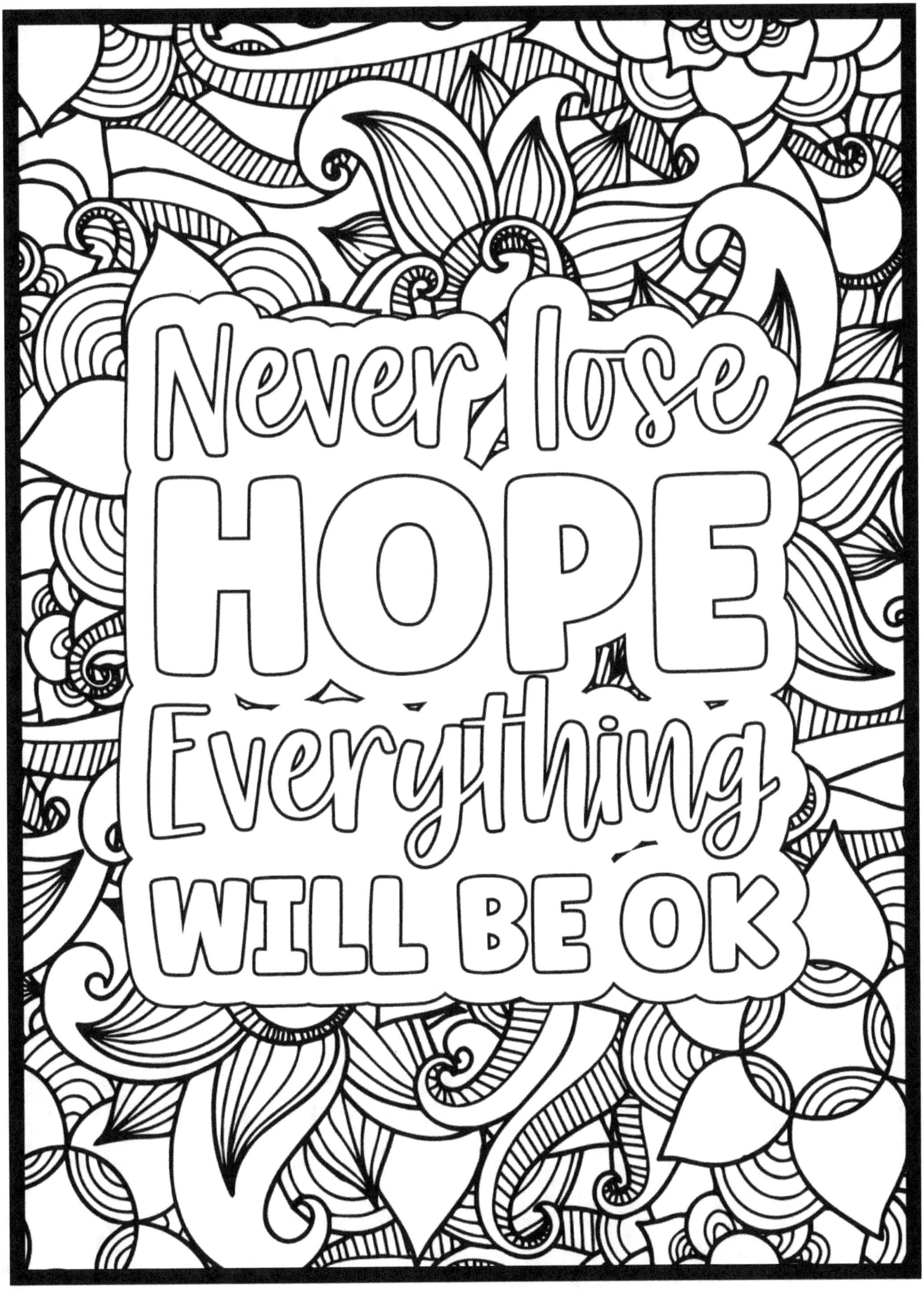
Never lose
HOPE
Everything
WILL BE OK

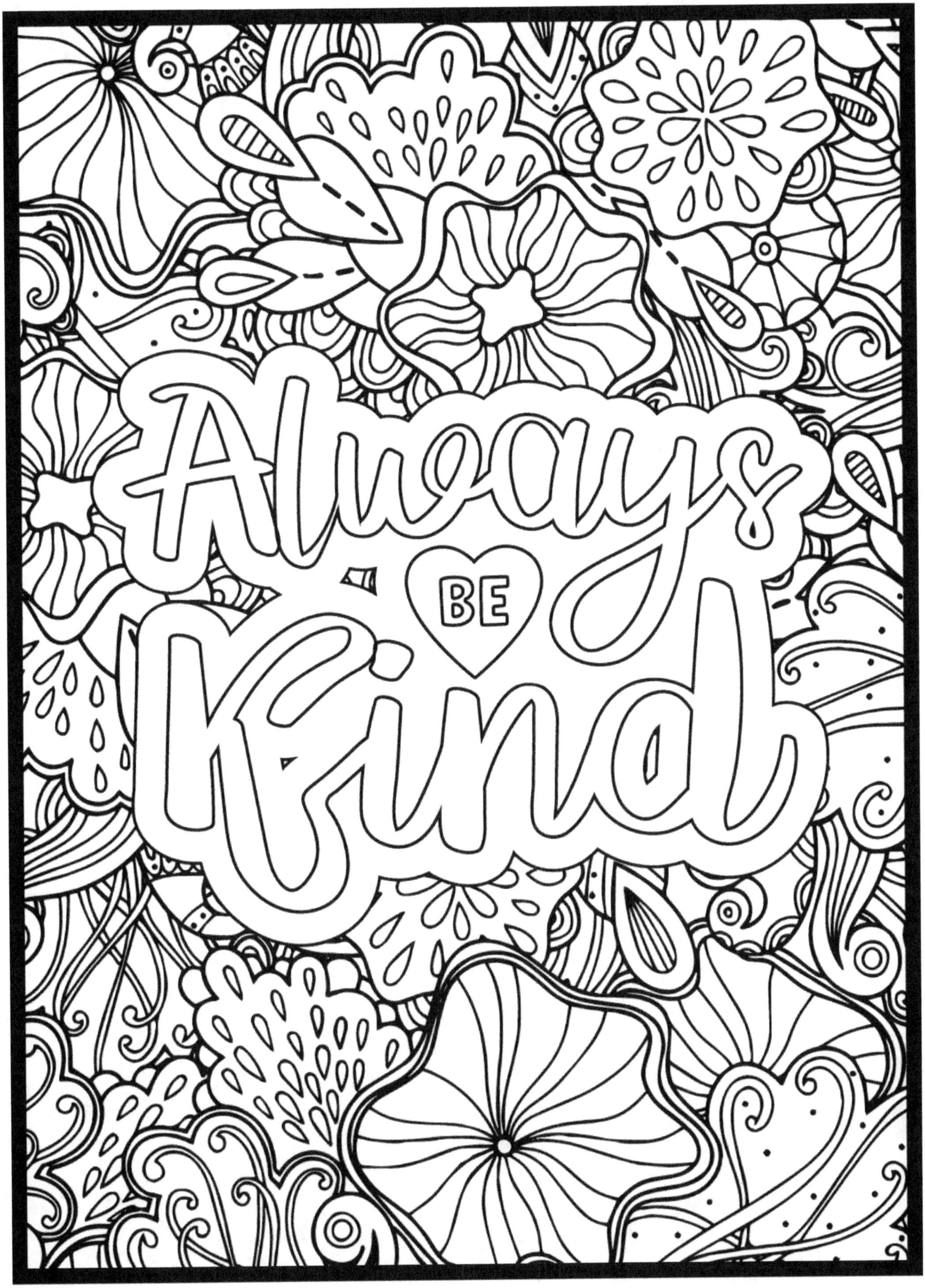
Always
BE
Kind

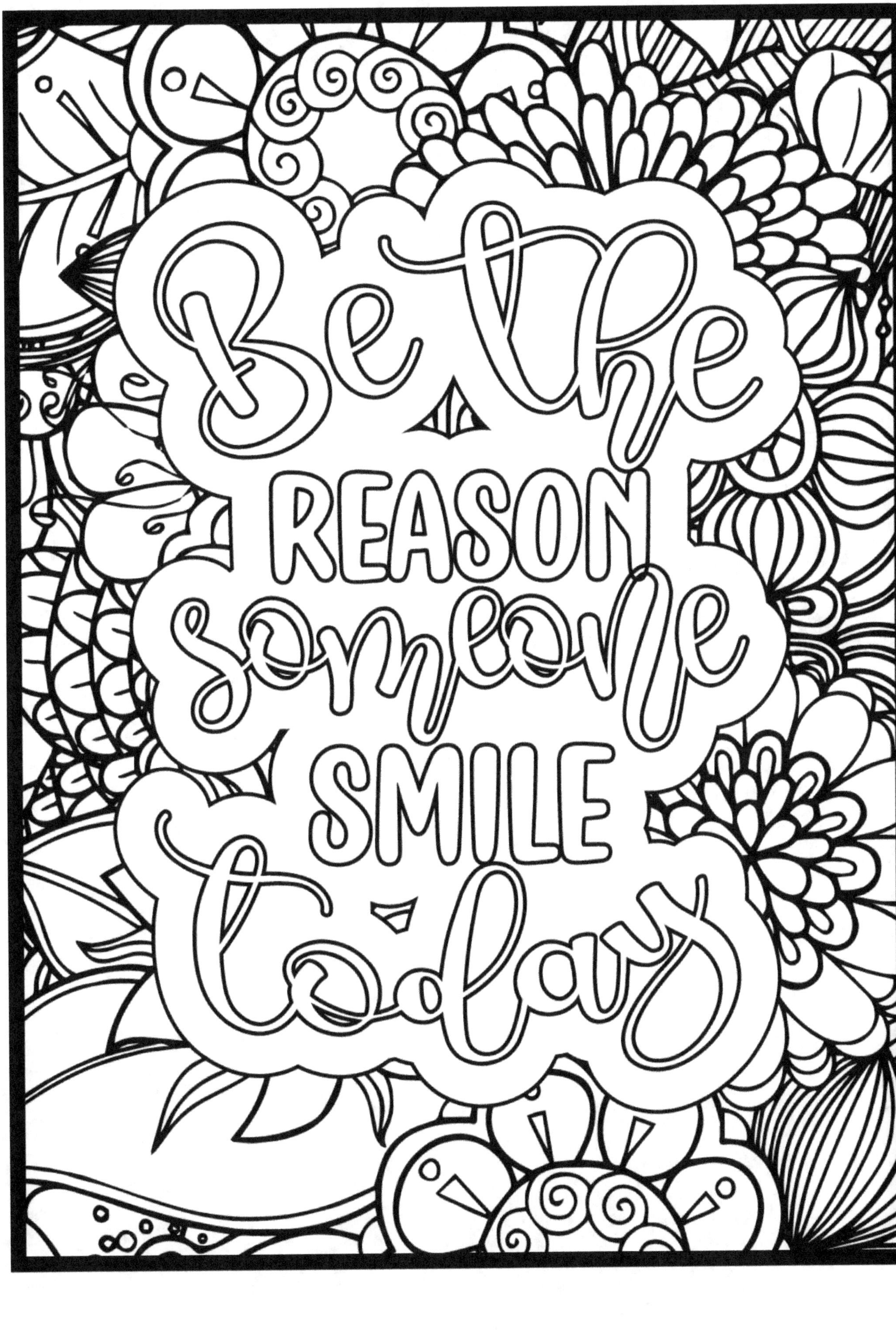
Be the
REASON
someone
SMILE
today

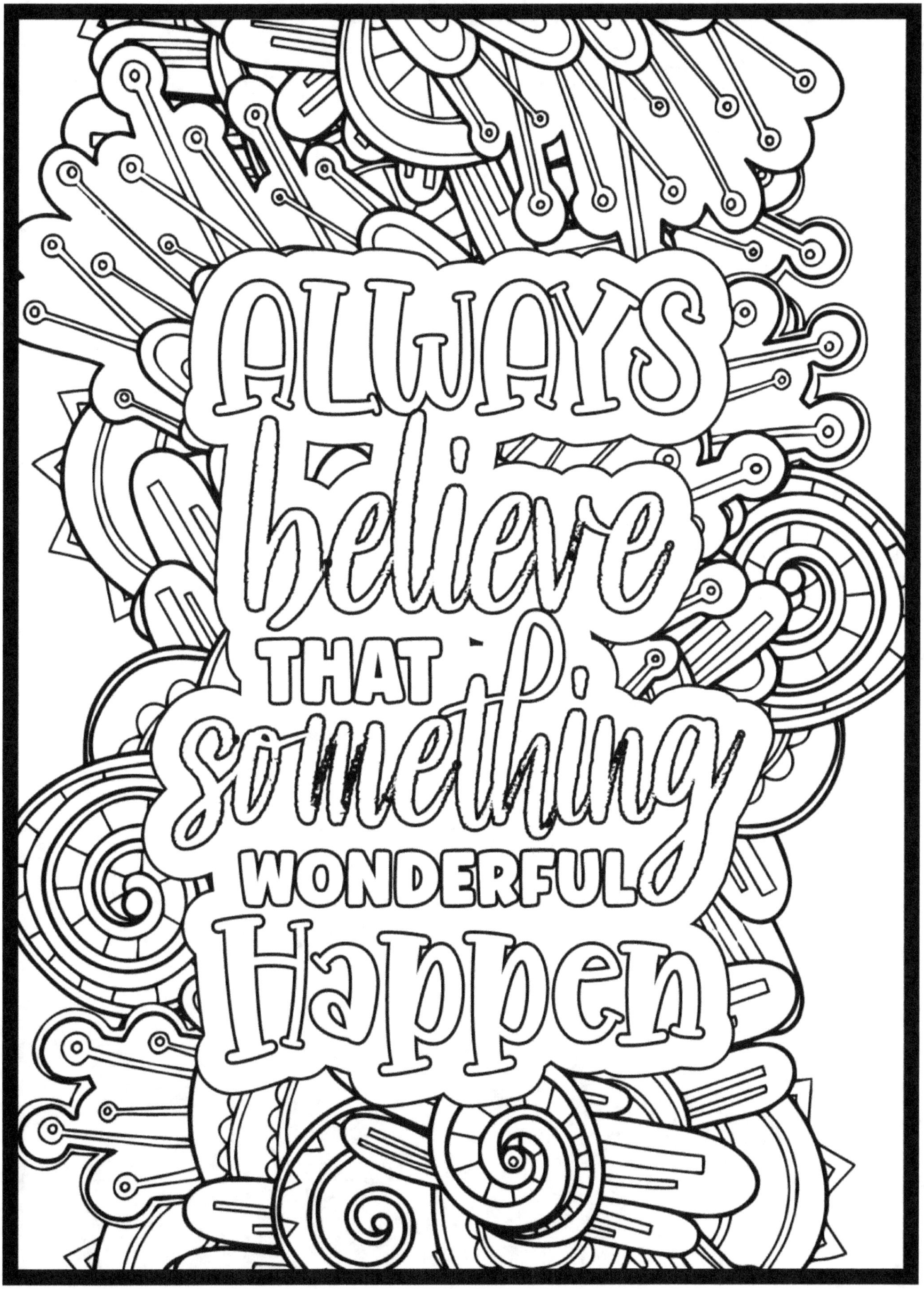
ALWAYS
believe
THAT
something
WONDERFUL
Happen

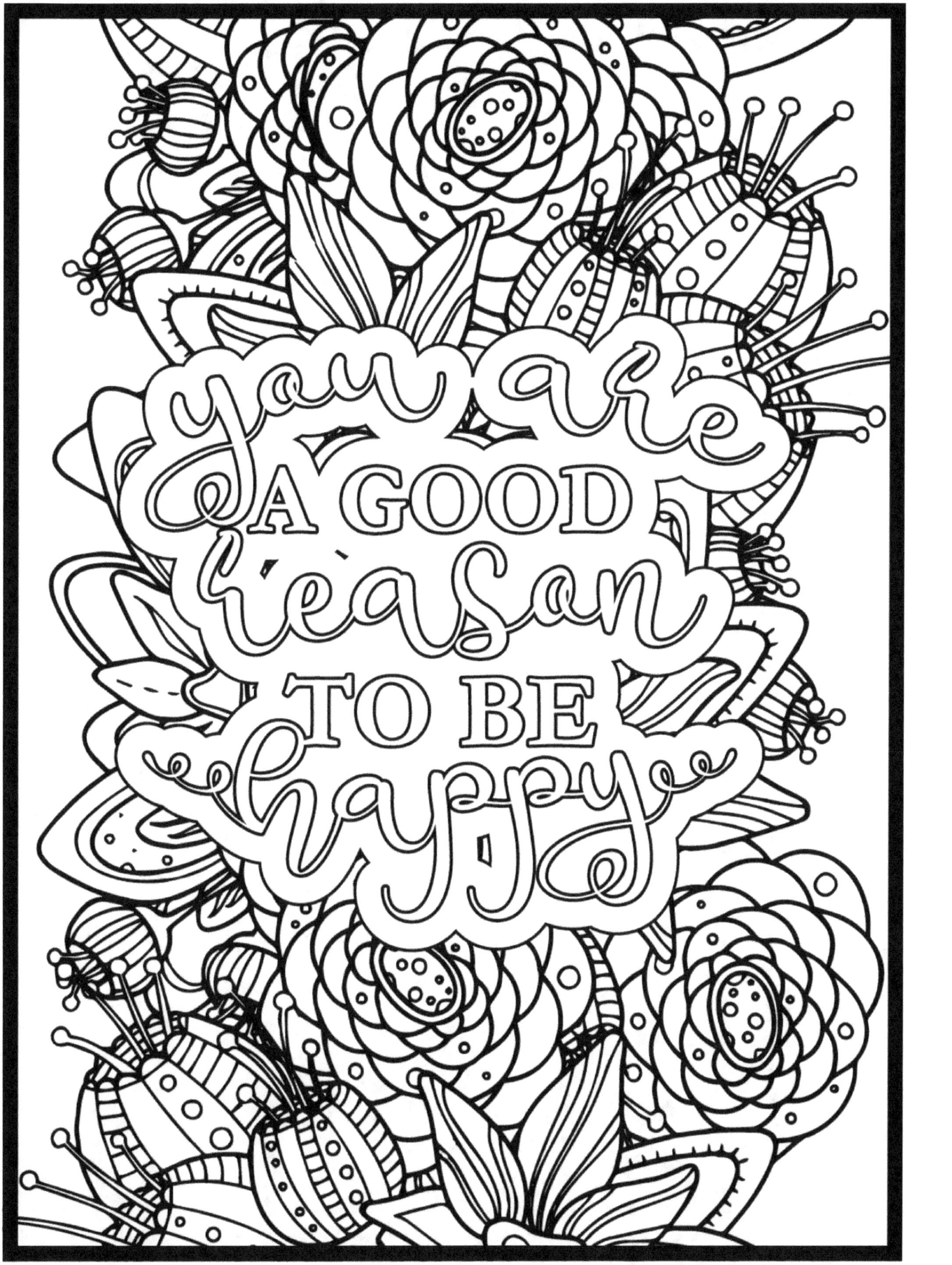
you are
A GOOD
reason
TO BE
happy

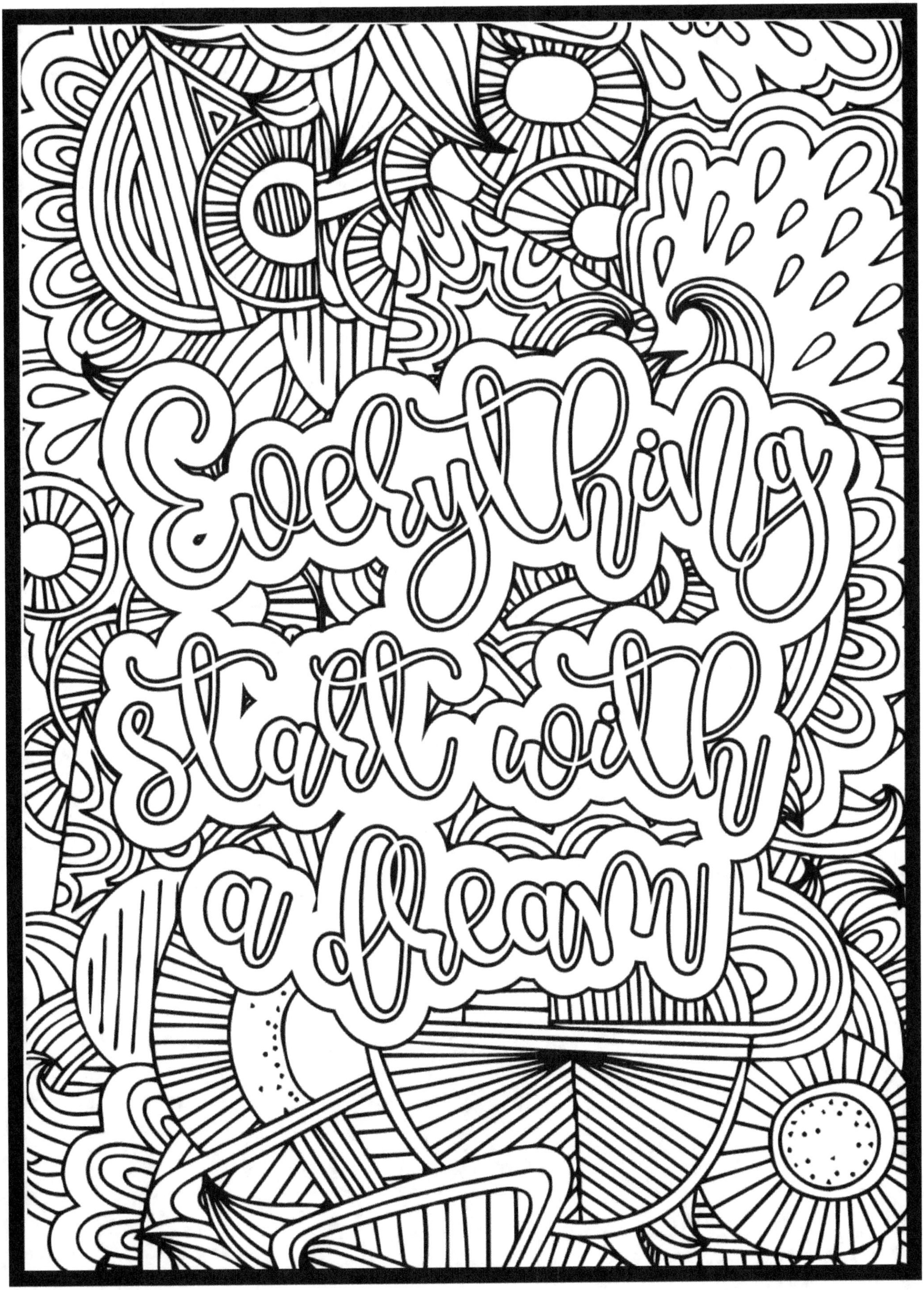
Everything
start with
a dream

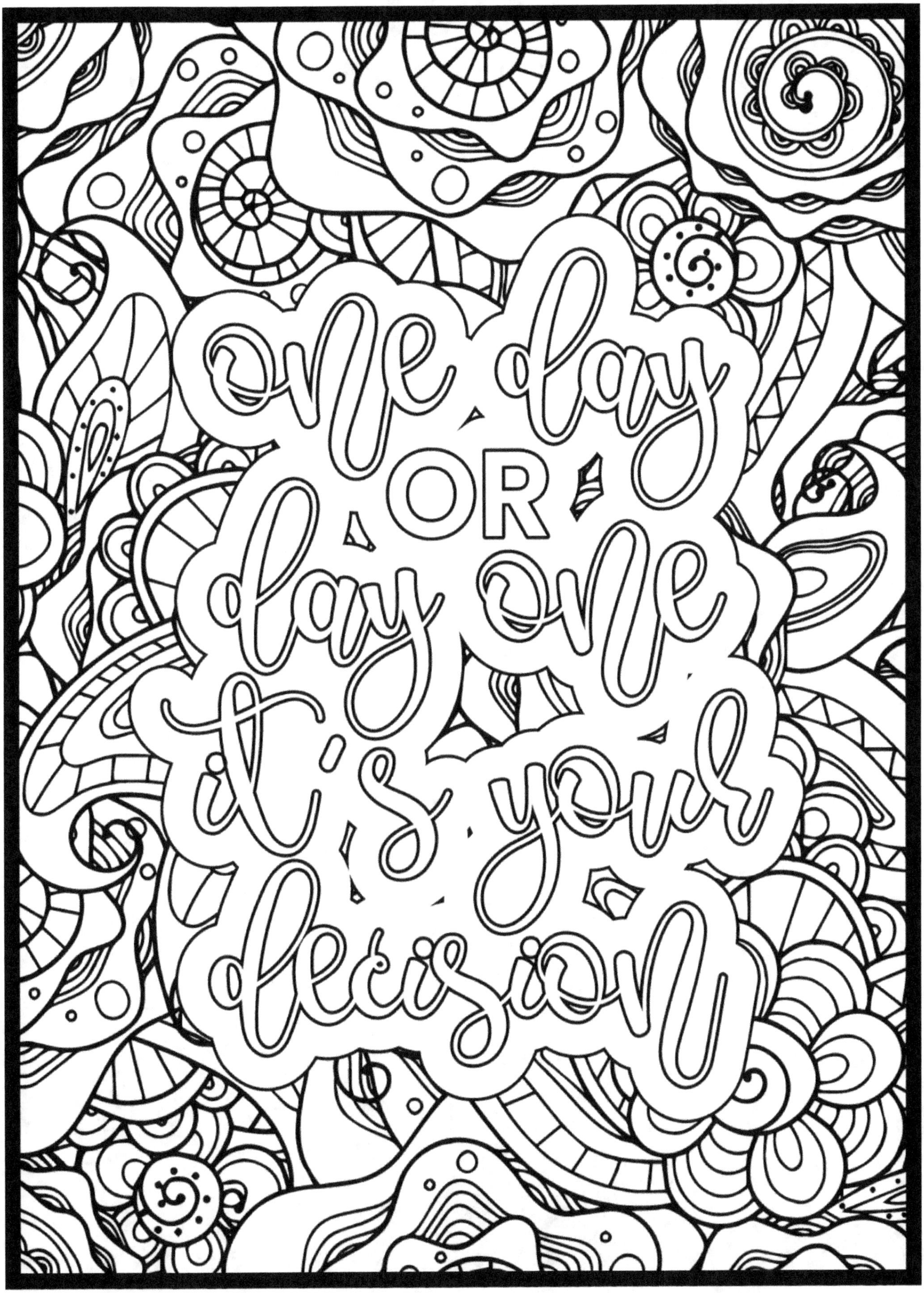
one day
OR
day one
it's your
decision

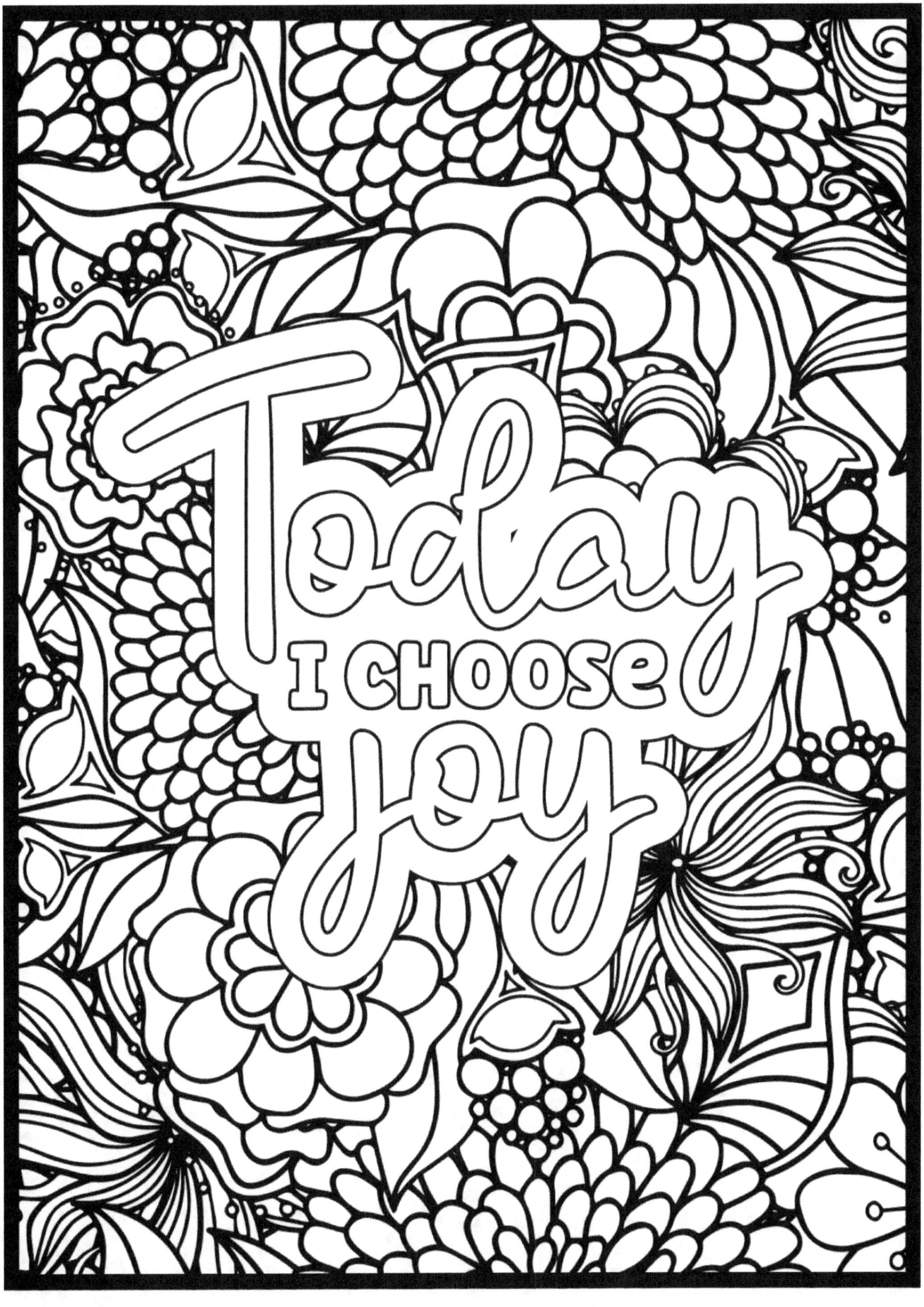
Today
I CHOOSE
joy

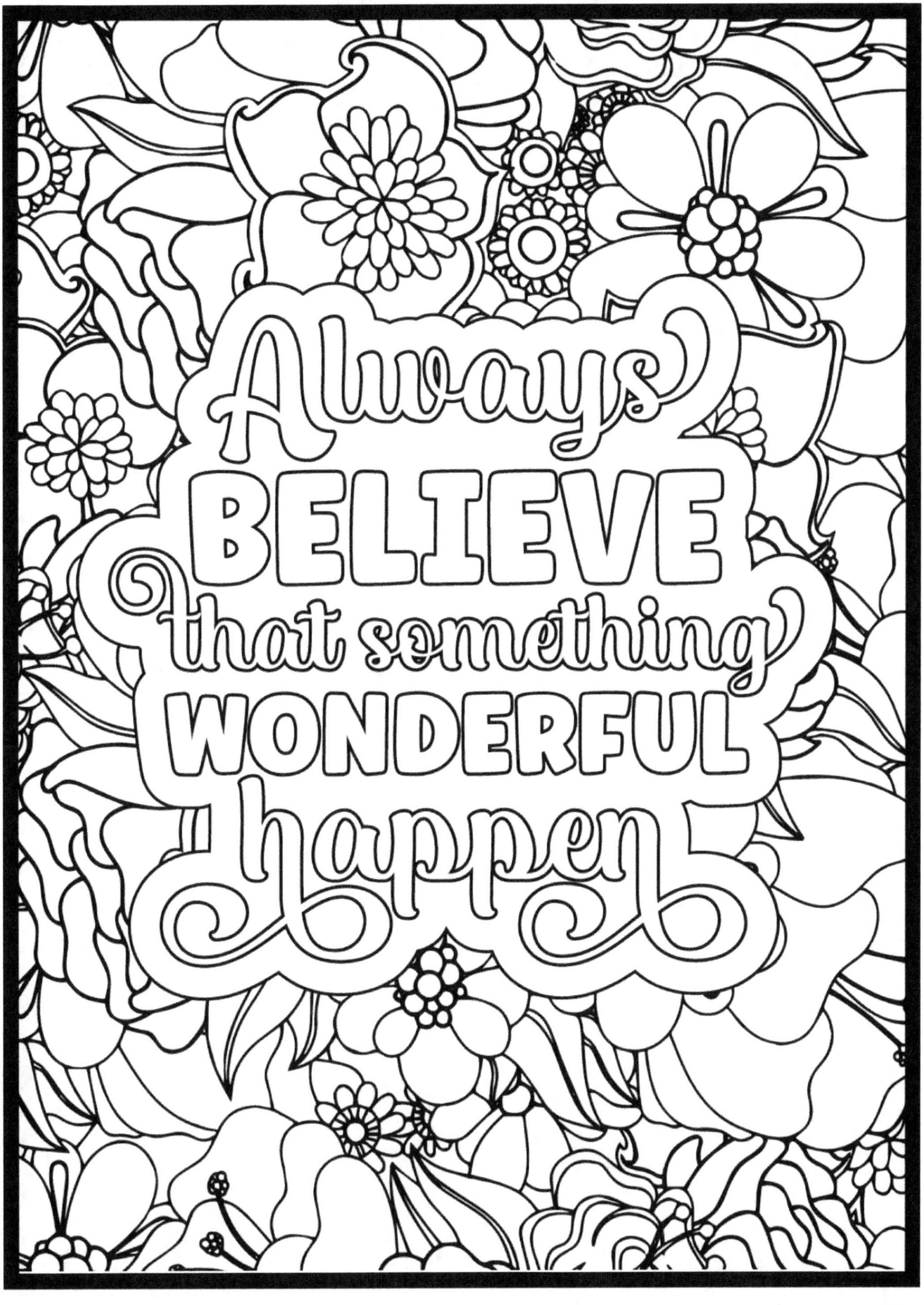
Always
BELIEVE
that something
WONDERFUL
happen

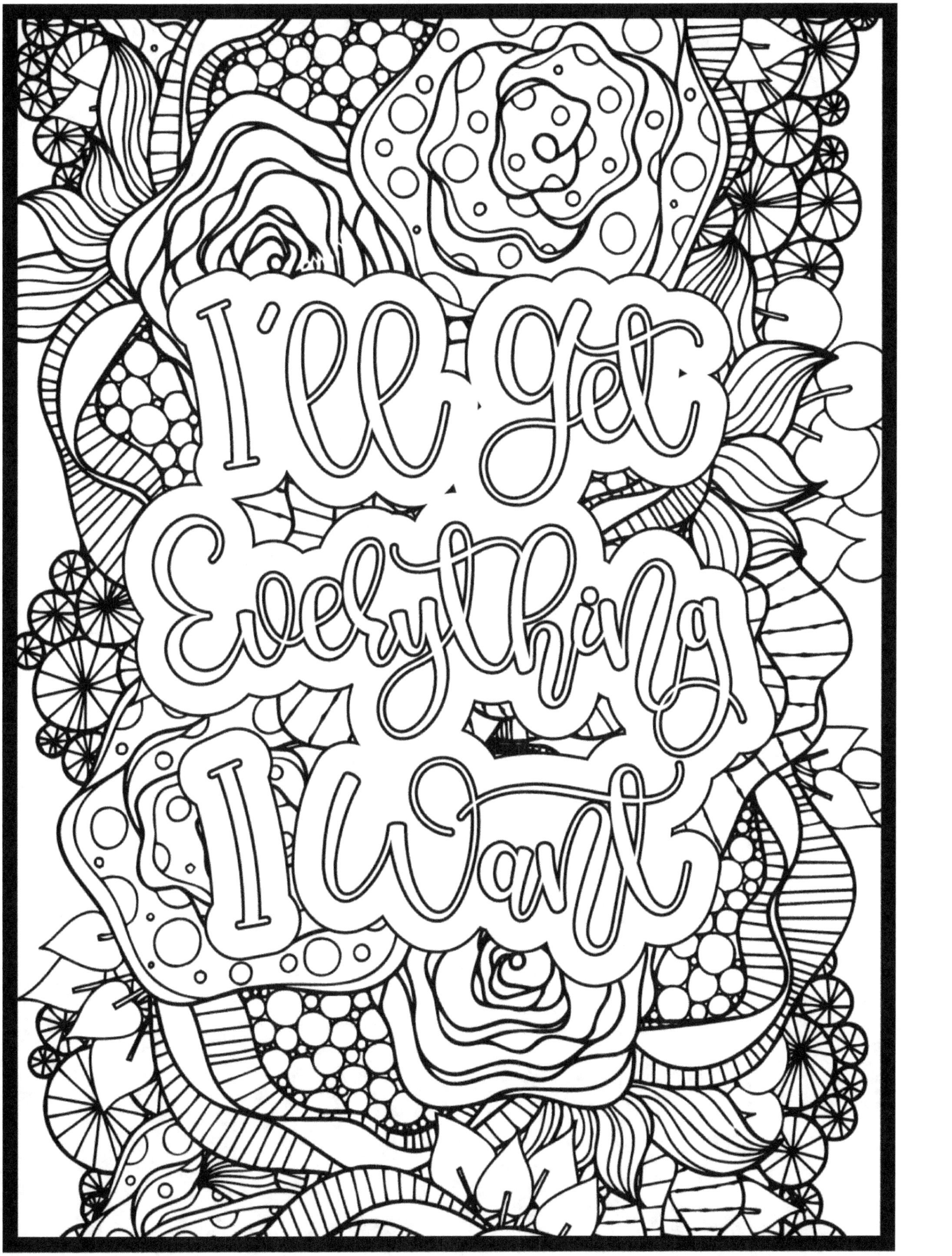
I'll Get
Everything
I Want

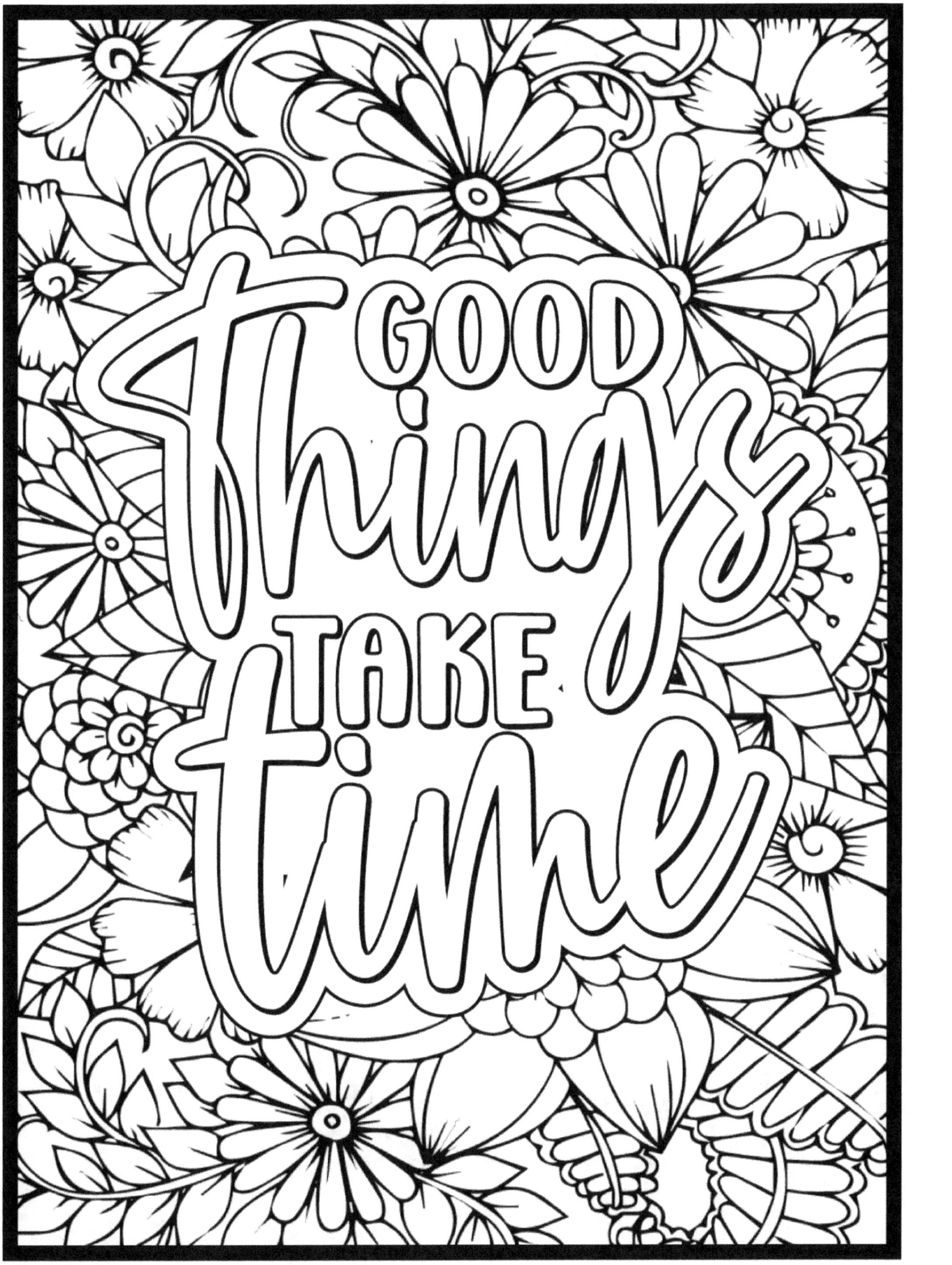
GOOD
things
TAKE
time

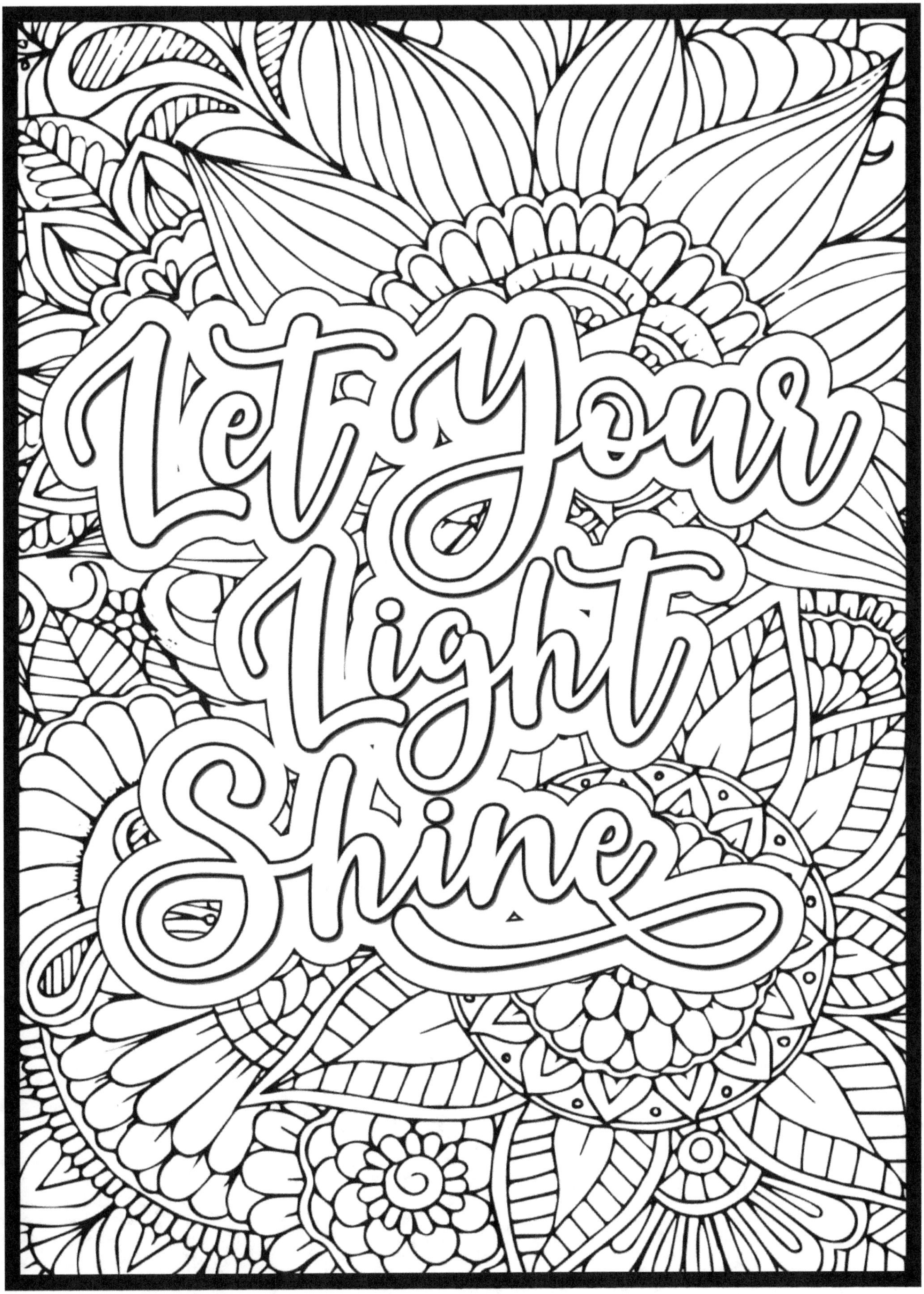
Let Your
Light
Shine

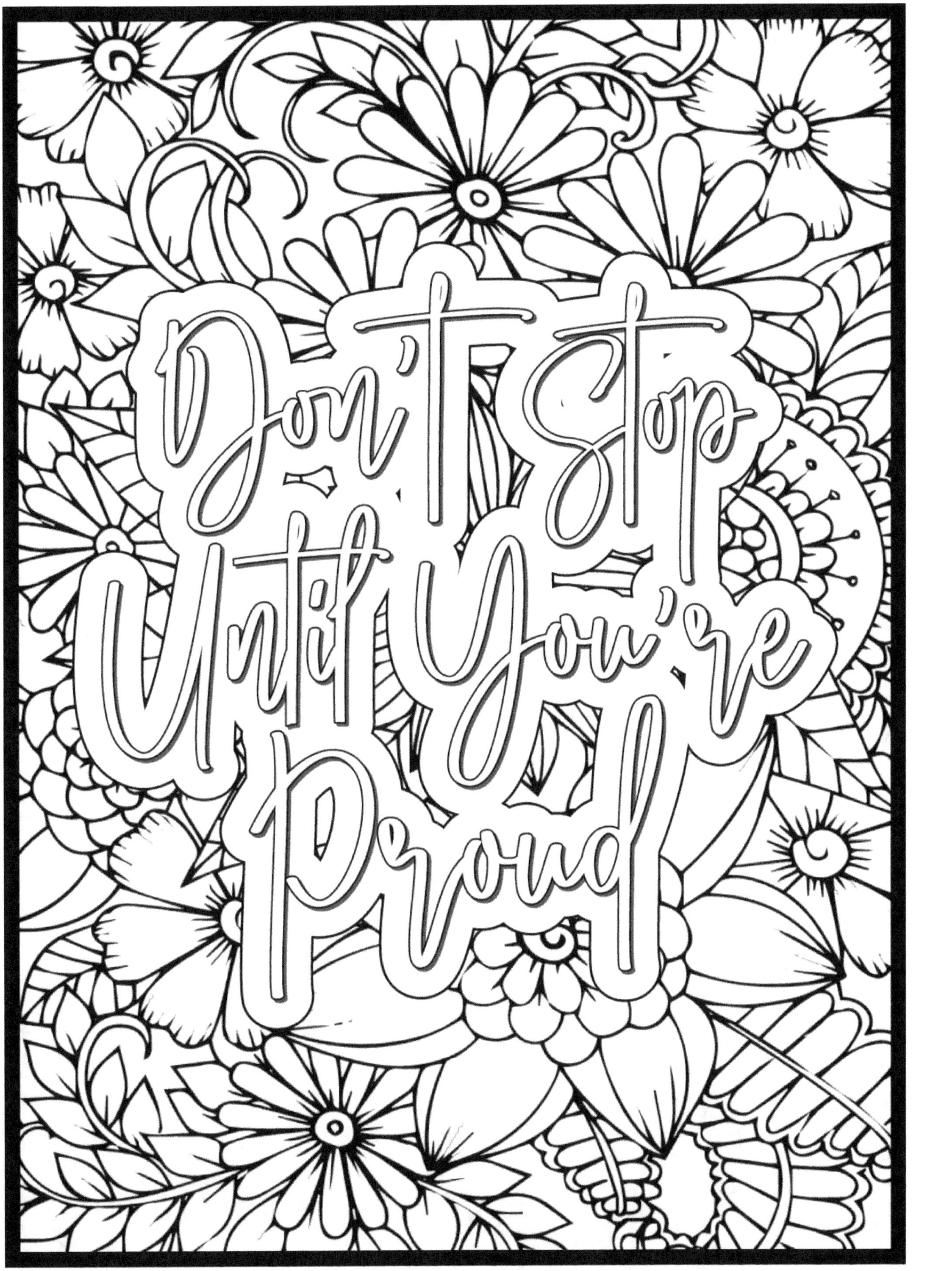
Don't Stop Until You're Proud

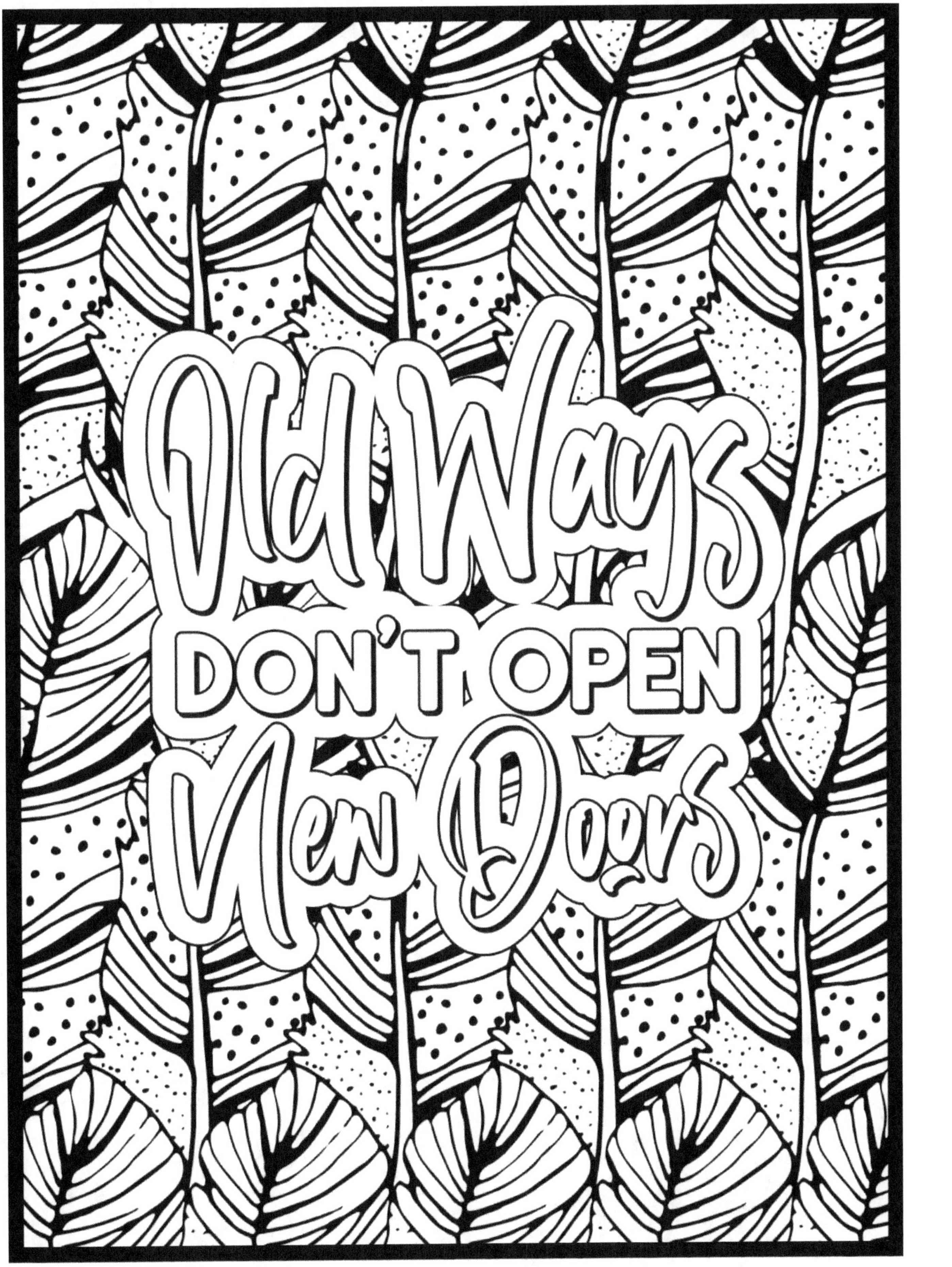
Old Ways
DON'T OPEN
New Doors

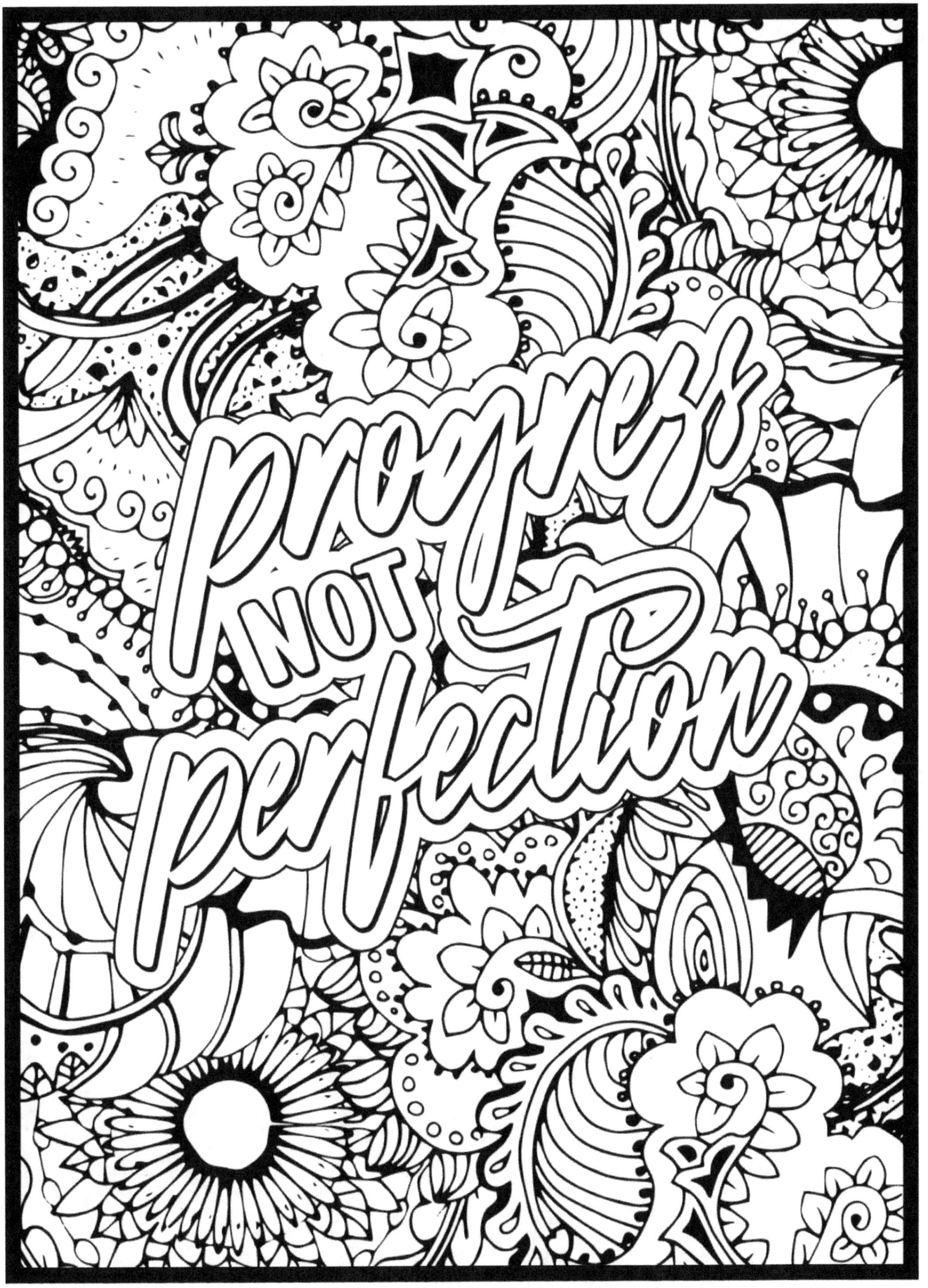
progress
NOT
perfection

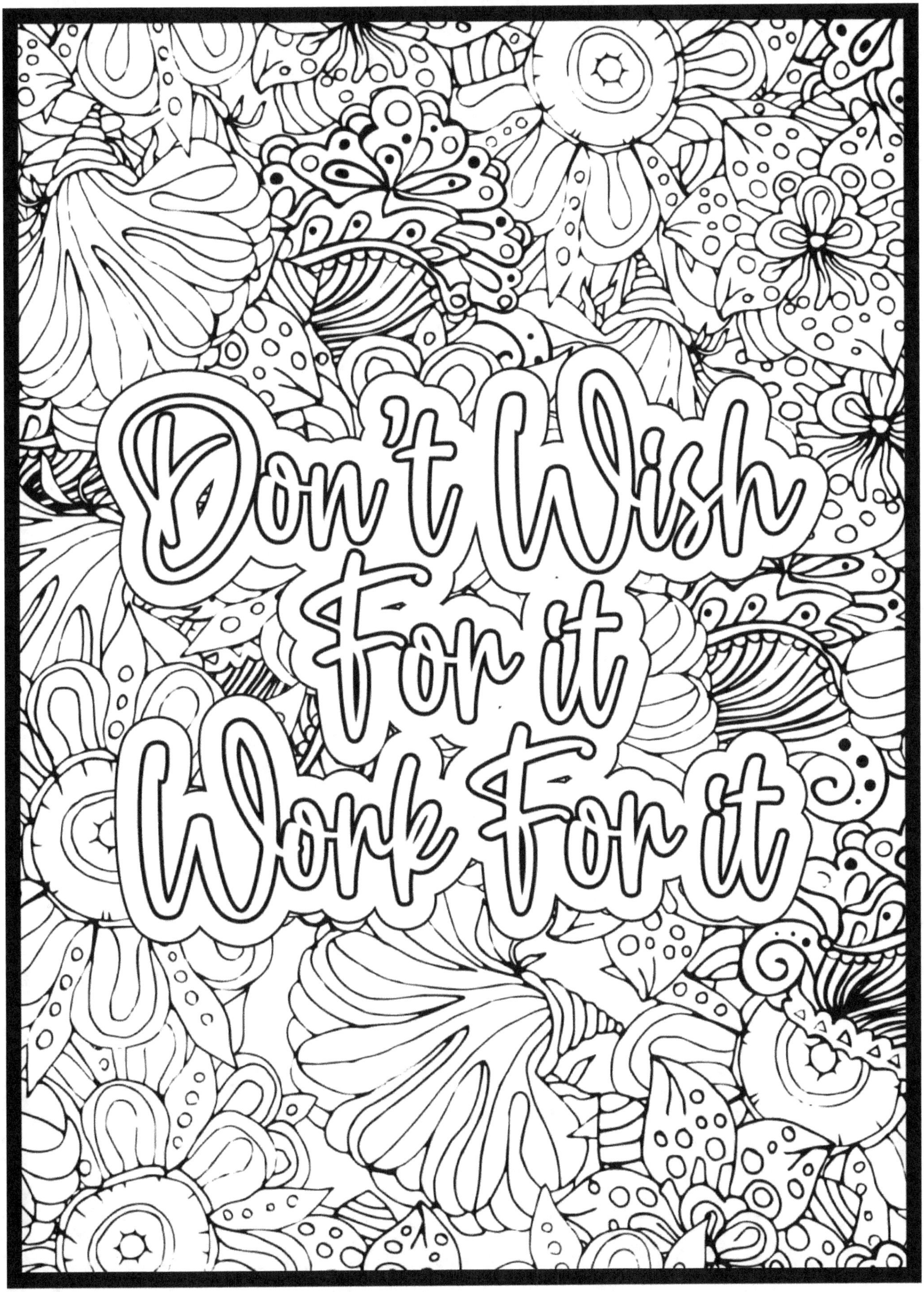
Don't Wish
For it
Work For it

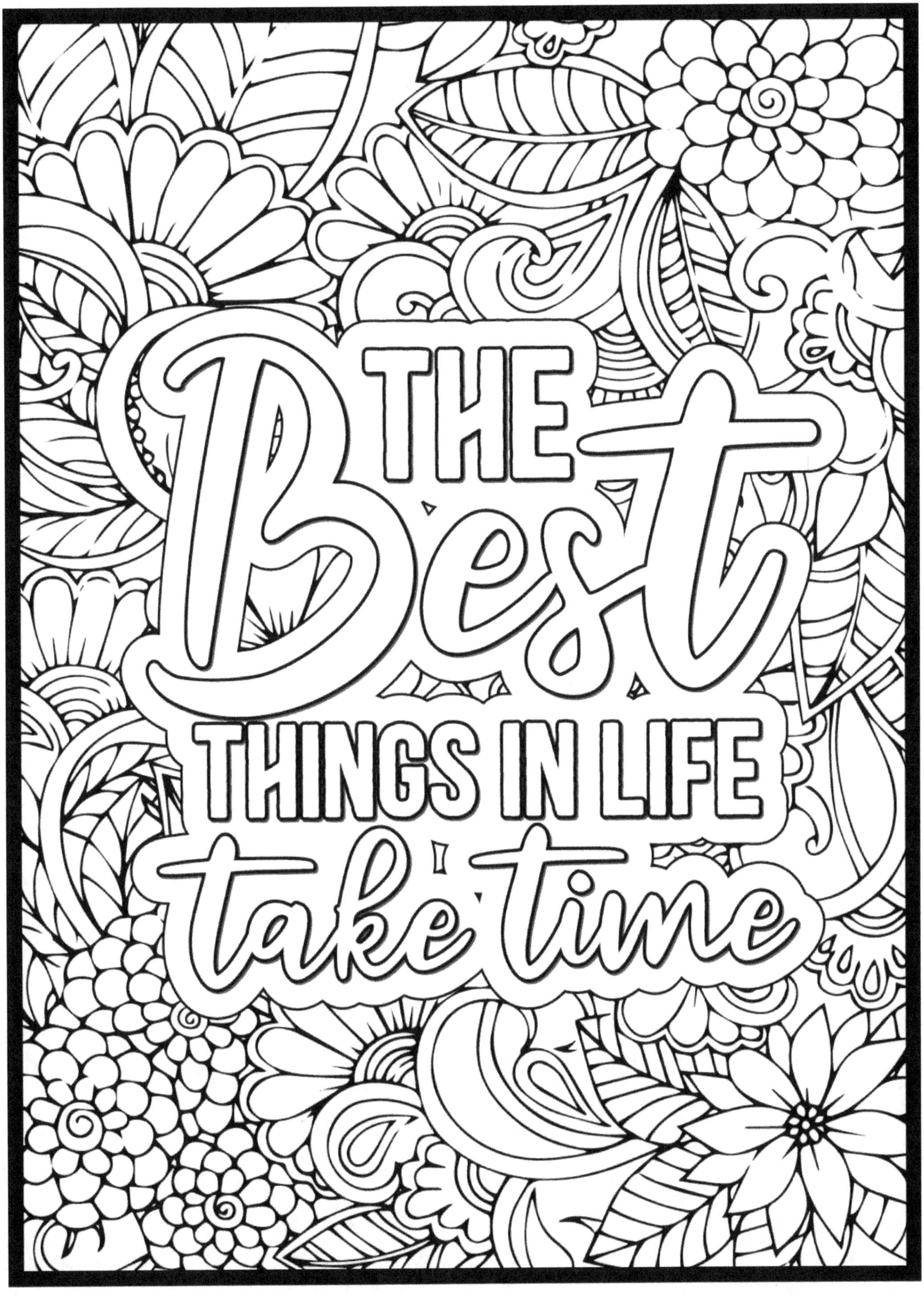
THE Best
THINGS IN LIFE
take time

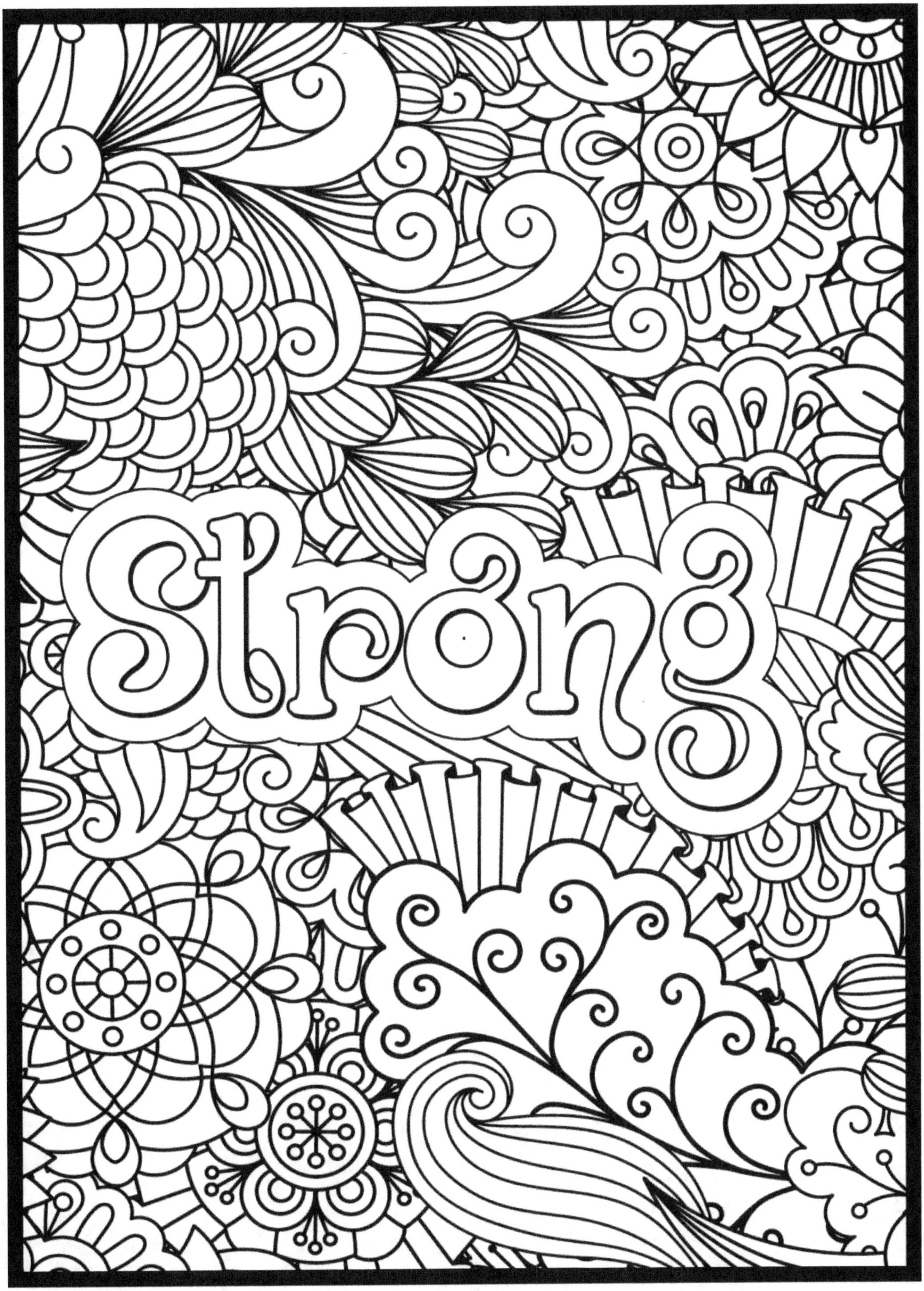
Strong

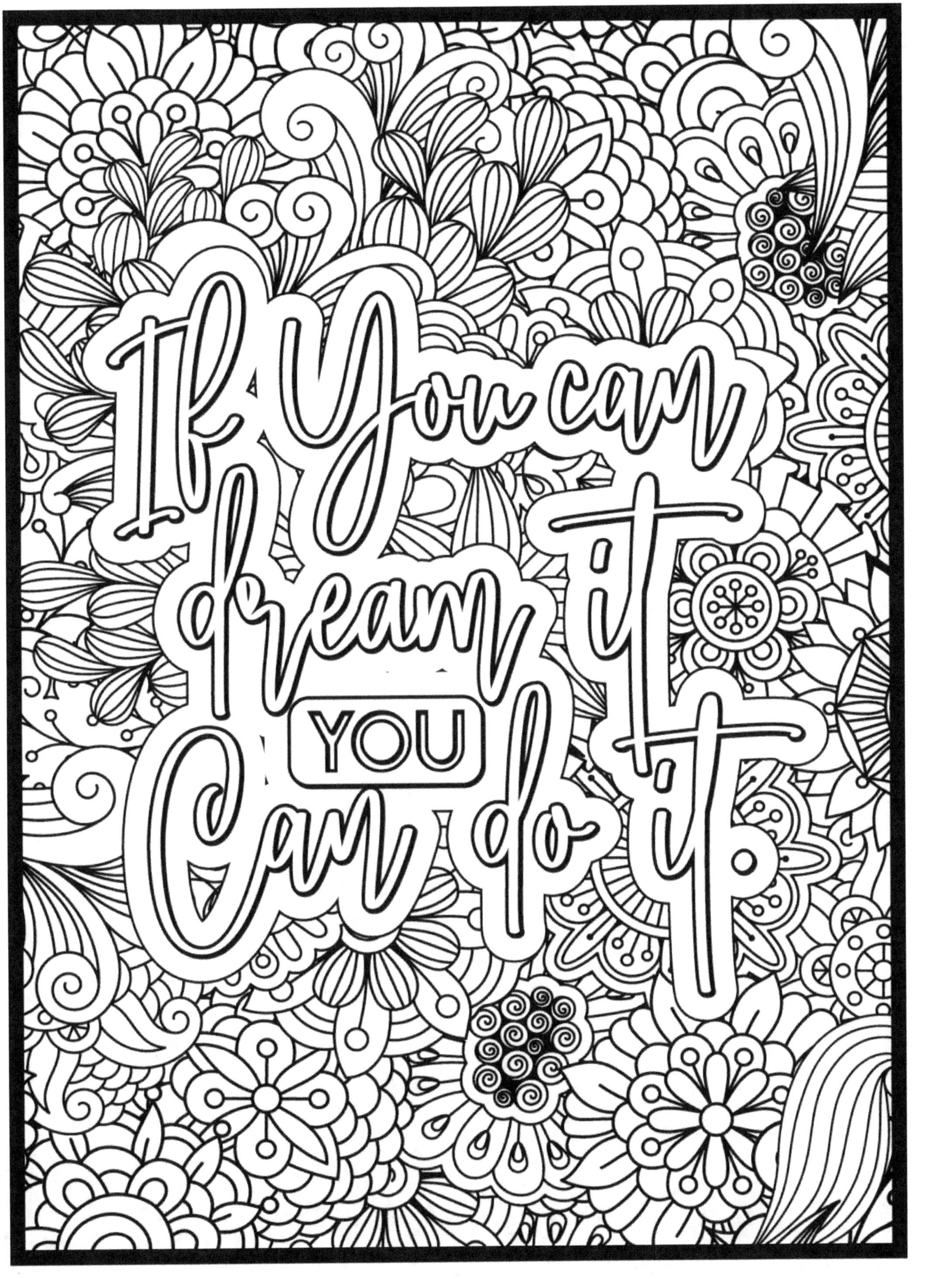
If You can dream it
YOU
Can do it

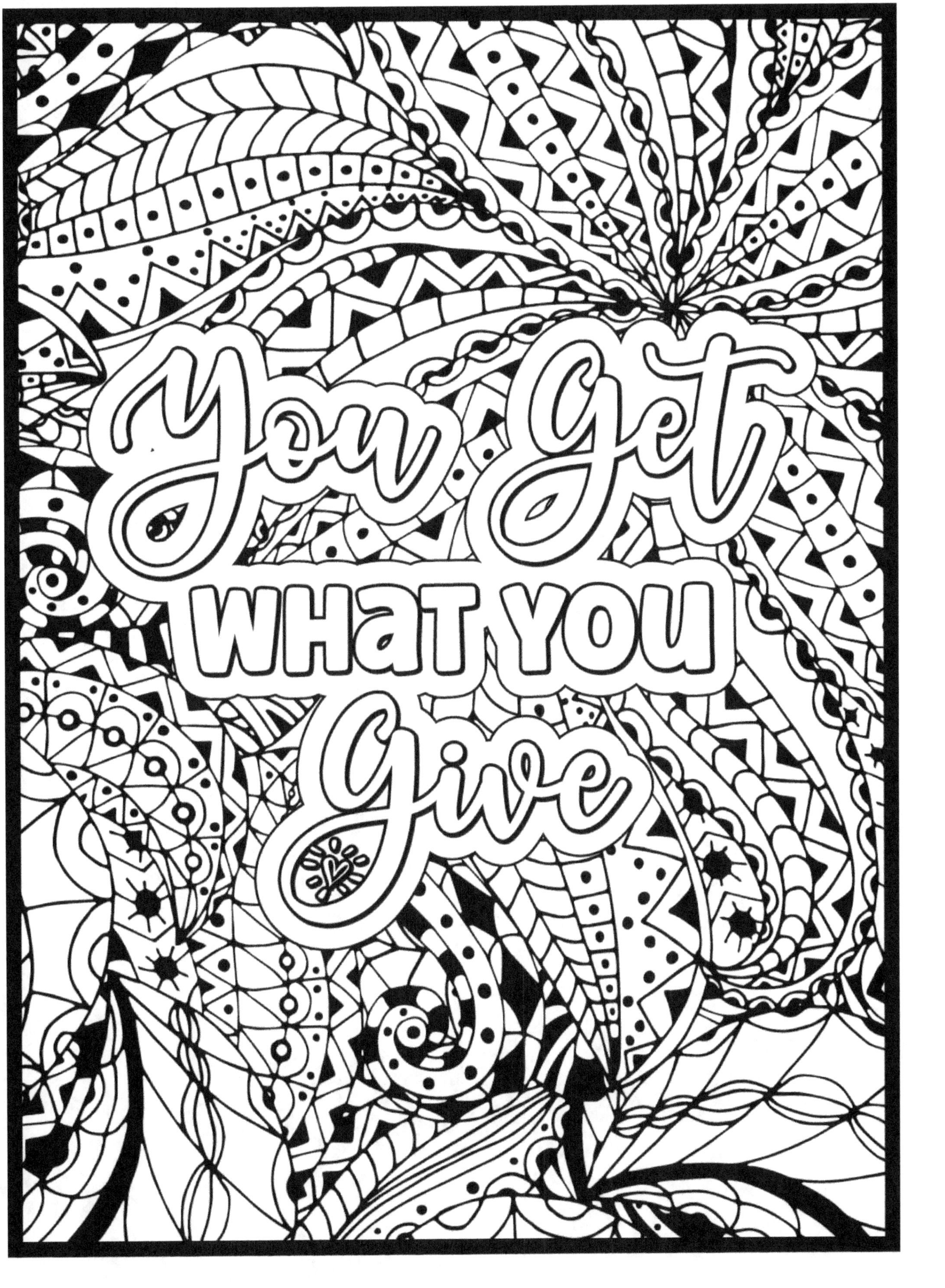
You Get
WHAT YOU
Give

www.ingramcontent.com/pod-product-compliance
Lightning Source LLC
Chambersburg PA
CBHW062011220526
45467CB00032BA/2377
9798386896560